MASTERMINDS Riddle Math *Series*

SKILLS BOOSTERS FOR THE RELUCTANT MATH STUDENT

Reproducible Skill Builders And Higher Order Thinking Activities Based On NCTM Standards

By Brenda Opie and Douglas McAvinn

Incentive Publications, Inc.
Nashville, Tennessee

Illustrated by Douglas McAvinn
Cover illustration by Douglas McAvinn

ISBN 0-86530-448-3

PRINTED IN THE UNITED STATES OF AMERICA
www.incentivepublications.com

TABLE OF CONTENTS

DETERMINING ORDER IN WHOLE NUMBERS

To whom do little pigs write? (Their pen pals) 1

What did Mama Corn say to Baby Corn when asked, "Mama, where did I come from?"
(The stalk brought you) 2

ROUNDING TO THE NEAREST WHOLE NUMBER

What would you eat to win a race? (You would eat fast food) 3

WRITING STANDARD NUMERALS

What did the homesick lizard say to his new friends? (Iguana go home) 4

FINDING THE CORRELATION BETWEEN MATH AND THE REAL WORLD

Exploring Math in the "Real" World 5

Searching for Numbers in the "Real" World and Numbers in Nature 6

ADDING WHOLE NUMBERS

What did the beaver say to the tree? (It's been nice gnawing you) 7

What keys don't open doors? (Turkeys, monkeys, and donkeys) 8

SUBTRACTING WHOLE NUMBERS

What's the difference between someone who's been sick too long and a pulled tooth?
(One is too thin and the other is tooth out) 9

What does a tuba call his grandfather? (Ooohm papa) 10

TARGET PRACTICE 11

If you had 10 oranges in one hand and 6 oranges in the other, what would you have?
(Awfully big hands) 12

What's another name for a cat burglar? (A purr-snatcher) 13

CORRELATING MATH WITH DAILY EXPERIENCES

Richer or Poorer? 14

Travels of *Flat Stanley* 15-16

IDEAS FOR MATH JOURNAL STARTERS

25 Math Journal Starters 17

MULTIPLYING WHOLE NUMBERS

Beat the Timer 18

Napier's Bones 19

Astounding Nines 20

Jumbled Number Facts 21

Multiplication Magic Squares 22

Multiplication Games 23-25

What do you find twice in "everyday", four times in "every week", and once in a "year"?
(You find the letter "e") 26

What do baby birds eat for dessert? (Chocolate chirp cookies) 27

Why do frogs have it made? (They eat what bugs them) 28

Multiplication Made Easy by Using the Lattice Method 29

DIVIDING WHOLE NUMBERS

If you cross Bambi with a ghost, what would you have? (You'd have bamboo) 30

What's the definition of a flood? (A river that's too big for its bridges) 31

How far do cows go through school? (Through cow-ledge) **32**
What do you call a dark horse? (A nightmare) **33**

USING A CALCULATOR FOR MIXED WHOLE NUMBER PRACTICE
Magic Potions **34**

PROBLEM SOLVING CHECKLIST and WORD PROBLEMS INVOLVING WHOLE NUMBERS
Problem Solving Checklist **35**
Why did Dracula go to the orthodontist? (To improve his bite) **36**

FACTORS, COMPOSITES, AND PRIMES
Rocket Boosters **37**
Prime or Composite? **38**
Prime Factor Bubble Magic **39**
The Slide Works!! **40**

FRACTION MANIPULATIVES AND GAMES
Making Fraction Kits (Part One) **41**
Let the Games Begin!! (Part Two) **42**

FRACTION SKILL ACTIVITIES
How is life like a shower? (One wrong turn and you're in hot water) **43**
What do bakers use as the main ingredient in dog biscuits? (They use collie-flour) **44**
What's a band director's favorite day of the year? (It's March fourth) **45**
What's the definition of an igloo? (An icicle built for two) **46**
What did the Martians say when they landed on Earth by mistake?
    (Sorry, we didn't planet this way) **47**
What continent do you see the first thing in the morning? (You see Europe) **48**
What did the man say when he became the father of triplets? (I can't believe my census) .. **49**
AND THE WINNER IS **50**

CONNECTING LANGUAGE ARTS WITH FRACTIONS
A Fraction Dictionary **51**

DECIMAL SKILL ACTIVITIES
What should you do if your dog starts to chew up your dictionary?
    (Take the words right out of his mouth) **52**
What do you call a cow eating grass? (A lawn moo-er) **53**
Cross Number Puzzle **54**
What happens when you put snakes on a car window? (You get windshield vipers) **55**
A Trick for Adding and Subtracting Decimals **56**
What happened when the canary flew into the fan? (Shredded tweet) **57**
Decimal Bingo **58**
What's the title of this picture? (A turtle on a skateboard) **59**
What did one escalator say to the other escalator?
    (I think I am coming down with something) **60**
What happened to the dog when he ate only garlic and onions?
    (His bark was worse than his bite) **61**

THINKING ACTIVITIES USING DECIMALS
Let's Play *JEOPARDY*! **62**

Road Kill Café Menu **63-64**

SOLVING PROPORTIONS AND RATIOS
What did one calendar say to the other calendar? (I have more dates than you do) **65**
Which president do monkeys like best? (Ape Lincoln) **66**

USING PERCENTS
Where do geologists go for entertainment? (To rock concerts) **67**
Who couldn't get their airplane to fly? (The Wrong Brothers) **68**
How does St. Peter greet you as you approach the gates? (Well, halo there) **69**

USING LOGIC
Movin' On! **70**

MEASURING ACTIVITIES
Measurement Man **71**
Student Recording Sheet **72**
Decisions, Decisions, Decisions **73**
What is the title of this picture? (A chicken on one crutch) **74**

GEOMETRY ACTIVITIES
Designing with Area **75**
Where's the best place to see a man-eating fish? (At a seafood restaurant) **76**
A Geometry Scavenger Hunt **77**
What did the doctor prescribe for the bald rabbit? (Hare tonic) **78**
What did the digital watch say to its mother? (Look ma, no hands) **79**

APPENDIX – CHARTS, GRIDS, AND WHOLE NUMBER FACTS SPEED TESTS **80**
Multiplication Facts **81**
A Table of Factors **82**
Grids **83-84**
Whole Number Speed Tests **85-88**

ANSWER KEY **89-91**

NAME _____

To whom do little pigs write?

DIRECTIONS: Solve each problem and locate your answer in the decoder at the bottom of the page. Each time your answer appears in the decoder, write the letter of the problem above it.

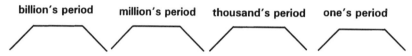

billion's period   million's period   thousand's period   one's period

703,958,416,123

Name the number in the:

1. Ten's place = _____ **N**
2. Hundred thousand's place = _____ **I**
3. Billion's place = _____ **A**
4. Thousand's place = _____ **E**
5. Hundred million's place = _____ **L**
6. Ten thousand's place = _____ **R**
7. Million's place = _____ **H**
8. Ten billion's place = _____ **S**
9. Hundred billion's place = _____ **T**
10. Ten million's place = _____ **P**

_7_ _8_ _6_ _4_ _1_   _5_ _6_ _2_   _5_ _3_ _9_ _0_

Determining order in whole numbers

NAME _____

What did Mama Corn say to Baby Corn when asked, "Mama, where did I come from?"

DIRECTIONS: Solve each problem and locate your answer in the decoder at the bottom of the page. Each time your answer appears in the decoder, write the letter of the problem above it.

1. Name the number that is 1 thousand greater than 5,239 = _____ U

2. Name the number that is 4 hundred greater than 999 = _____ L

3. Name the number that is 2 thousand less than 35,782 = _____ H

4. Name the number that is 10 thousand less than 586,832 = _____ R

5. Name the number that is 100 thousand greater than 7,640 = _____ O

6. Name the number that is 2 million less than 2,684,000 = _____ B

7. Name the number that comes 1 before 100,000 = _____ G

8. Name the number that is "halfway" between 9,000 and 10,000 = _____ A

9. Name the number that comes 1 before 1,000,000 = _____ E

10. Name the number that is "halfway" between 6,500 and 7,000 = _____ T

11. Name the number that is 2 thousand greater than 49,600 = _____ K

12. Name the number that is 10 billion less than 13,678,000,000 = _____ Y

13. Name the number that comes 1 before 30,000 = _____ S

6,750	33,782	576,832	107,640	999,999		29,999	6,239	107,640	33,782	99,999	6,239	684,000	3,678,000,000	6,750

51,600   1,399   9,500   6,750   S   29,999   6,239   107,640   33,782   99,999   6,239   684,000   3,678,000,000   6,750

2

NAME _____

What would you eat to win a race?

DIRECTIONS: First, round each of the numbers in the problems below. Second, find your answer in the decoder at the bottom of the page. Third, each time your answer appears in the decoder, write the letter of the problem above it.

1. Round 75,420 to the nearest ten thousand = _____ A

2. Round 75,420 to the nearest hundred = _____ Y

3. Round 75,420 to the nearest thousand = _____ D

4. Round 75,420 to the nearest ten = _____ L

5. Round 293,678,432 to the nearest ten = _____ T

6. Round 293,678,432 to the nearest hundred = _____ W

7. Round 293,678,432 to the nearest ten thousand = _____ F

8. Round 293,678,432 to the nearest thousand = _____ E

9. Round 293,678,432 to the nearest hundred thousand = _____ O

10. Round 293,678,432 to the nearest ten million = _____ S

11. Round 293,678,432 to the nearest million = _____ U

| 75,400 | 293,700,000 | 294,000,000 | 293,678,400 | 293,700,000 | 294,000,000 | 75,420 | 75,000 |

| 293,678,000 | 80,000 | 293,678,430 | 293,680,000 | 80,000 | 290,000,000 | 293,678,430 |

| 293,680,000 | 293,700,000 | 293,700,000 | 75,000 |

NAME _____

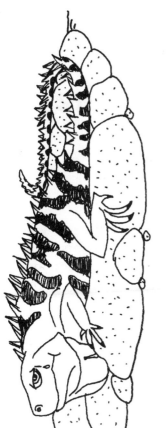

What did the homesick lizard say to his new friends?

DIRECTIONS: Write the standard numeral for each expanded notation. Find your answer in the decoder and each time your answer appears in the decoder, write the letter of the problem above it.

1. seven million, two hundred forty thousand, six = _____ E

2. forty-two billion, three hundred sixty-four million, thirty thousand, four hundred = _____ M

3. two hundred seventy-seven billion, six hundred forty-three million, two hundred thousand, six = _____ H

4. seventy billion, twenty-four thousand, sixty = _____ O

5. forty-two million, three hundred sixty-four thousand, thirty-four = _____ N

6. two hundred seventy-seven thousand, six hundred forty-three = _____ A

7. seven billion, two hundred forty million, six hundred thousand = _____ U

8. two hundred seventy-seven million, six hundred forty-three thousand, six hundred = _____ G

9. seventy thousand, two hundred forty-six = _____ I

70,246	277,643,600	7,240,600,000	277,643	42,364,034	277,643

277,643,600	70,000,024,060	277,643,200,006	70,000,024,060	42,364,030,400	7,240,006

Exploring Math in the "Real" World

Background Information: By relating math concepts to the real world, students can have a "hook" by which to internalize math concepts. Also, students have a reason for learning about numbers, fractions, percentages, measurement, etc. if they can see a connection to real-life situations or objects.

When introducing concepts such as fractions, ask students to think of the many, varied, and unusual places fractions can be found in the "real" world. Make a classroom chart and leave it up while studying fractions.

A sample list from one middle grade's classroom included the following:

1. weight of sports equipment
2. football statistics- 5½ yd. line
3. rain gauge
4. weighing food
5. jewelry sizes
6. measuring utensils
7. road signs
8. nutrient listings on food boxes
9. stock market
10. airport signs
11. dividing food
12. shutter release on a camera
13. division of seats at a stadium
14. manicure or pedicure
15. sale discounts
16. ingredients in kitty litter
17. taxes
18. shoe sizes
19. science lab equipment
20. scale of miles on a map
21. military artillery
22. tape sizes
23. pencil sizes- 2½
24. art supplies
25. microscopes
26. fabric measurements
27. thickness of pizza
28. weather forecasting
29. rulers
30. menus
31. bakeries
32. cartoons
33. tire sizes
34. light years in space
35. chef shows on TV
36. movie footage
37. voltage of batteries
38. medicine prescriptions
39. voting polls
40. test papers
41. glasses' sizes
42. braces' sizes
43. sizes of clothes
44. jail sentence
45. computer games
46. billboards
47. telling time

This activity took approximately 30 minutes. Each student then illustrated 4 of his/her favorites. This introductory lesson is also very effective when introducing decimals, percentages, standard measurement, geometry and other math

Searching for Numbers in the "Real" World

DIRECTIONS: Think of the many, varied, and unusual places that numbers can be found in our daily lives. Try to think of at least 10. The first one has been done for you.

1. 1 dozen red roses
2. _____
3. _____
4. _____
5. _____
6. _____
7. _____
8. _____

9. _____
10. _____
11. _____
12. _____
13. _____
14. _____
15. _____
16. _____

Numbers in Nature

MATERIALS: Plastic bag, pencil, clipboard, colored pencils or crayons
DIRECTIONS: Take a nature hike around your school with members of your class. While on your hike, look for examples of numbers in nature. For example, an acorn cracked in half could indicate the number two. A four-leaf clover could indicate the number four. A tree branch with nine twigs could indicate the number nine, and a mosquito's legs could indicate the number six. Whenever possible, collect samples of your finds, or if it is not practical to actually collect the "real" thing, make a drawing on this recording sheet. You'll probably be amazed at how many representations of numbers you can find all around you.

Use this space to sketch some of the natural things you located. Be sure to indicate what you have drawn and the numbers that your drawings represent.

Name _____

What did the beaver say to the tree?

DIRECTIONS: Examine the method used in completing an addition problem. Look at the example given on the right. You might want to think of this method as "**stack addition**" since you are stacking the numbers before you actually add.

```
   43
 +38
  11 (3 + 8)
 +70 (40 + 30)
  81
```

Solve each of the problems below and then find your answer in the decoder. Each time the answer occurs in the decoder, write the letter of the problem above it.

1. 34
   +76

   = A

2. 564
   +318

   = W

3. 57
   +98

   = U

4. 45
   +45

   = T

5. 146
   +285

   = I

6. 29
   +37

   = N

7. 347
   +163

   = B

8. 892
   + 60

   = S

9. 83
   +65

   = Y

10. 83
   +71

   = C

11. 48
   +95

   = G

12. 485
   + 63

   = O

13. 92
   +39

   = E

431	90	952	
510	131	131	66
	66	431	154	131

| 143 | 66 | 110 | 882 | 431 | 66 | 143 | | 148 | 548 | 155 |

NAME _____

What keys don't open doors?

DIRECTIONS: Solve each problem and locate your answer in the decoder at the bottom of the page. Each time your answer appears in the decoder, write the letter of the problem above it.

Example
Add.
Regroup when necessary.

$$\begin{array}{r} {\scriptstyle 1\ 1\ \ 1} \\ 12{,}681 \\ +37{,}823 \\ \hline 50{,}504 \end{array}$$

1. $\begin{array}{r} 645 \\ +132 \\ \hline \end{array}$ = A

2. $\begin{array}{r} 36 \\ +73 \\ \hline \end{array}$ = D

3. $\begin{array}{r} 402 \\ +486 \\ \hline \end{array}$ = N

4. $\begin{array}{r} 319 \\ +268 \\ \hline \end{array}$ = O

5. $\begin{array}{r} 7{,}413 \\ +2{,}656 \\ \hline \end{array}$ = M

6. $\begin{array}{r} 1{,}713 \\ +1{,}611 \\ \hline \end{array}$ = S

7. $\begin{array}{r} \$1{,}688.39 \\ 432.78 \\ +\ \ \ 84.22 \\ \hline \end{array}$ = Y

8. $\begin{array}{r} 8{,}679 \\ 1{,}921 \\ +4{,}015 \\ \hline \end{array}$ = E

9. $\begin{array}{r} \$17.39 \\ 1.65 \\ +\ \ .08 \\ \hline \end{array}$ = K

10. $\begin{array}{r} 408 \\ 36 \\ +12 \\ \hline \end{array}$ = R

11. $\begin{array}{r} \$37.03 \\ .82 \\ +16.25 \\ \hline \end{array}$ = U

12. $\begin{array}{r} 34{,}675 \\ +\ 1{,}934 \\ \hline \end{array}$ = T

36,609	$54.10	456	$19.12	14,615	$2,205.39	3,324

10,069	587	888	$19.12	14,615	$2,205.39	3,324

777	888	109

109	587	888	$19.12	14,615	$2,205.39	3,324

NAME _____

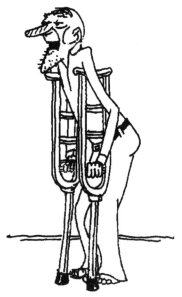

What's the difference between someone who's been sick too long and a pulled tooth?

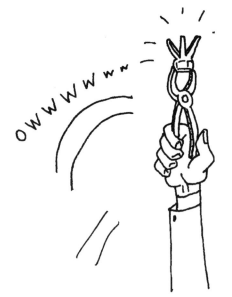

DIRECTIONS: Solve each problem below and find your answer in the decoder. Each time your answer appears in the decoder, write the letter of the problem above it.

1. _____ + 12 = 30 (N)

2. _____ + 8 = 23 (R)

3. 38 + _____ = 65 (A)

4. 19 + _____ = 85 (S)

5. _____ + 40 = 96 (H)

6. 13 + _____ = 87 (U)

7. 27 + _____ = 103 (D)

8. _____ + 11 = 34 (I)

9. 88 + _____ = 153 (E)

10. _____ + 92 = 147 (O)

11. 15 + _____ = 28 (T)

‾55‾ ‾18‾ ‾65‾   ‾23‾ ‾66‾   ‾13‾ ‾55‾ ‾55‾   ‾13‾ ‾56‾ ‾23‾ ‾18‾

‾27‾ ‾18‾ ‾76‾   ‾13‾ ‾56‾ ‾65‾   ‾55‾ ‾13‾ ‾56‾ ‾65‾ ‾15‾

‾23‾ ‾66‾   ‾13‾ ‾55‾ ‾55‾ ‾13‾ ‾56‾   ‾55‾ ‾74‾ ‾13‾

What does a tuba call his grandfather?

DIRECTIONS: Using graph paper you can make solving subtraction problems easier. Study the example below and then solve each problem. Find your answer in the decoder. Each time your answer occurs in the decoder, write the letter of the problem above it. A four-step example has been done for you.

Subtract ones
```
            3  12
   6  8  4̶  2̶
-  3  4  9  3
               9
```

Subtract tens
```
         7  13 12
   6  8̶  4̶  2̶
-  3  4  9  3
            4  9
```

Subtract hundreds
```
         7  13 12
   6  8̶  4̶  2̶
-  3  4  9  3
         3  4  9
```

Subtract thousands
```
         7  13 12
   6  8̶  4̶  2
-  3  4  9  3
      3  3  4  9
```

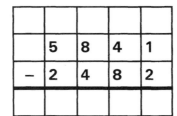

```
   6  3  4  5
-     6  5  7
```
1. _____ = (P)

```
   5  8  4  1
-  2  4  8  2
```
2. _____ = (M)

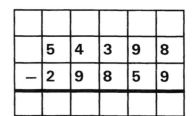

```
   5  4  3  9  8
-  2  9  8  5  9
```
3. _____ = (A)

```
   5  8  0  7
-  3  9  2  8
```
4. _____ = (H)

```
   7  0  9  2
-  1  8  8  9
```
5. _____ = (O)

5,203   5,203   5,203   1,879   3,359   5,688   24,539   5,688   24,539

TARGET PRACTICE

Objective: To practice estimating numbers, subtracting, and strategizing

Number of players: 2-4 players

Materials: A deck of cards with jokers and picture cards removed

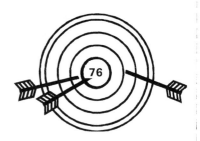

Directions: Shuffle the cards. The dealer deals each player four cards face down. Then the dealer turns over two more cards. The first card goes in the ten's place and the second on in the one's place. Together these two cards from the TARGET number. **See example to the right.**

Now, each player turns up four of their cards and arranges them into 2-digit numbers. Each player's strategy should include arranging his cards so that when the two numbers are either subtracted or added, he comes as close to the TARGET number as possible. For example, Player A and Player B have four cards to arrange. How would you (Player A) arrange these cards to arrive at the TARGET number?

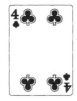   

Some possibilities are: $42 + 68 = 110$, or $24 + 68 = 92$, or $86 - 24 = 62$. If the last arrangement of cards is chosen as the best strategy to use, Player A subtracts the 62 from the TARGET number, 76, and the answer is 14. It is then Player B's turn to show his best strategy with his 4 cards. Whichever player is the closest to the TARGET number wins that round and gives himself 1 point.

For the next round, two new cards are turned up to form the TARGET number. Players can choose to use the same four cards or take four new cards from the deck. After 5 rounds, the player with the most points is the winner.

Other variations:

1. *Allow students to play in teams and work for a low group score.*

2. *Encourage students to try a 3-digit TARGET number and deal six cards for each player.*

3. *After students have become comfortable with playing the game, they may enjoy trading cards as one of their strategies in trying to get closest to the TARGET number.*

4. *Encourage students to creatively determine other ways to play the TARGET number.*

If you had 10 oranges in one hand and 6 oranges in the other, what would you have?

DIRECTIONS: Solve each problem and locate your answer in the decoder at the bottom of the page. Each time your answer appears in the decoder, write the letter of the problem above it.

EXAMPLE:

    2 13 8 10
    ~~33,905~~
  - 14,321
    19,584

1. 3,482
    - 1,351
        = S

2. 789
    - 342
        = D

3. 7,500
    - 726
        = N

4. 505
    - 98
        = H

5. $98.41
    - $63.20
        = G

6. 52,000
    -13,004
        = I

7. 1,000
    - 537
        = B

8. 52,001
    - 49,502
        = Y

9. 200
    -197
        = L

10. 983,618
    -212,504
        = U

11. 830
    - 443
        = F

12. 40,002
    - 35,803
        = W

13. $102.34
    - 1.23
        = A

$101.11	4,199	387	771,114	3	3	2,499

463	38,996	$35.21

407	$101.11	6,774	447	2,131

Adding and subtracting with regrouping

NAME _____

What's another name for a cat burglar?

DIRECTIONS: First, solve each problem below. Second, find your answer in the decoder at the bottom of the page. Third, each time your answer appears in the decoder, write the letter of the problem above it.

1. 6,875
   - 5,943
   _____
   = R

2. 4,007
   - 1,196
   _____
   = N

3. 1,072
   +3,451
   _____
   = C

4. 2,700
   - 1,836
   _____
   = E

5. 643
    21
    82
   + 56
   _____
   = U

6. 3,865
   - 1,766
   _____
   = T

7. 7,000
   - 5,541
   _____
   = A

8. 346
    78
    232
   + 135
   _____
   = H

9. $3.59
    1.56
    3.09
    .43
   + 7.18
   _____
   = S

10. $4.23
    .98
    7.65
   + .33
   _____
   = P

1,459	$15.85	2,811	2,099	802	4,523	791	864	932

$13.19	1,459	932	932	—	932

Richer or Poorer

Background Information: If each letter in your name were given a dollar value, how valuable would your name be? Use the code below and your calculator to determine the value of your name and the names of four other classmates or family members. Notice that the vowels are worth more than the consonants. Be prepared to round the average value of each letter to the nearest cent.

A = $30	H = $6	N = $11	T = $16
B = $1	I = $30	O = $30	U = $30
C = $2	J = $7	P = $12	V = $21
D = $3	K = $8	Q = $13	W = $17
E = $30	L = $9	R = $14	X = $18
F = $4	M = $10	S = $15	Y = $19
G = $5			Z = $20

An example has been done for you.

Tom Cruise = $16 + $30 + $10 + $2 + $14 + $30 + $30 + $15 + $30 = $177. Now, average the value of each letter by dividing the dollar total by the number of letters. *Tom Cruise* has 9 letters. $177 ÷ 9 = $19.66666, or $19.67. The average per letter for *Tom Cruise's* name is $19.67. **Using your calculator find out how valuable your name is and what the average is per letter.**

Your name _____ Total value _____ Average amount for each letter _____

Choose 4 other friends or family members and see who has the most valuable name by adding and then averaging your totals!

1. **Name** _____ Total value _____ Average amount for each letter _____

2. **Name** _____ Total value _____ Average amount for each letter _____

3. **Name** _____ Total value _____ Average amount for each letter _____

4. **Name** _____ Total value _____ Average amount for each letter _____

Name of the person whose average showed that his/her name was the most valuable:

_____

NAME _____

Correlating literature with math skills of measurement, addition, and subtraction

Travels of Flat Stanley

Materials: Book- *Flat Stanley* by Jeff Brown, large United States map, yarn, push pins, and outline of Flat Stanley. Clothes can be drawn on with markers or crayons; clothing should reflect where Flat Stanley is going to travel.

Days 1 and 2- Read *Flat Stanley* orally to your class. Students decide where they want to send Flat Stanley. They then need to draw clothing onto the character and cut him out. He will later be put in an envelope with a letter.

Day 3- Review letter writing skills and parts of a friendly letter. Students will write a letter to friends or relatives in other states asking them to take Flat Stanley somewhere interesting in their community. Students ask the receiver of their letters to take a photograph of Flat Stanley and return it with a brief summary of his travels.

During the rest of the school year, students can share their letters and photos as they receive them. A special Flat Stanley wall in your classroom can become the display area for the photographs and letters that are sent back to your students. Students can mark the city on a large classroom map where Flat Stanley was sent and use yarn to connect it back to their city. Students can also measure distances and record them on a chart next to the classroom map.

Sample questions students can answer about their classroom chart:

1. *How much farther did John's Flat Stanley travel than Jennifer's?*

2. *Add total round trip miles traveled by Megan's Flat Stanley.*

3. *Which state was visited most by Flat Stanleys?*

Bonus: What was the average number of miles traveled by Flat Stanley?

Example of classroom chart:

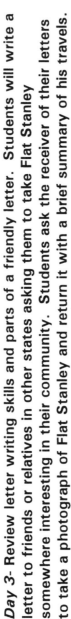

	Student's Name	City and State	Distance Traveled
1.	Jennifer M.	Topeka, Kansas	1,346 miles
2.			
3.			
4.			
5.			
6.			
7.			
8.			
9.			
10.			

25 Math Journal Starters

DIRECTIONS: If you have difficulty deciding what to write about in your math journal, the ideas below may be helpful in getting you started:

1. One thing I learned today.....

2. I completed .....

3. I explained to my friend.....

4. I made a connection when.....

5. I feel best about math when.....

6. I drew a picture and it helped me understand.....

7. One of the easiest ways for me to learn how to solve math word problems is.....

8. Something I did well.....

9. A new strategy that worked for me today.....

10. Something in math I would like to learn is.....

11. Something I did to help.....

12. I graphed.....

13. One thing in math I don't understand is.....

14. I explored a new math idea today by.....

15. A skill in math that I need to work harder to learn.....

16. I discovered a pattern.....

17. I estimated.....

18. I made.....

19. When I find an answer to something that was difficult for me, I feel.....

20. We worked in cooperative groups today, and as a team we discovered.....

21. The best part about math is.....

22. The worst part about math is.....

23. When we act out a story problem I.....

24. If I were the teacher in my math class, I would....

25. One of my best problem solving strategies is.....

BEAT THE TIMER
(A New Approach to Flash Cards)

MATERIALS: Blank cards 2" x 3" (a 4" x 6" index card cut in two), markers that will not show through on the unwritten side of the card, and a small sand timer.

DIRECTIONS: On one card write the problem *(example: 9 x 6)*. On the second card write the answer *(example: 54)*. It's best to write large numbers with a marker checking to see that the ink does not show through on the back of the card.

EXAMPLE:

Problem Card

9
x 6

Answer Card

54

GAME 1: Place all Problem Cards face up on one side of the desk or table. Place Answer Cards face up on the other side of the desk or table. Set the timer and begin matching Problem Cards with Answer Cards. The object is to complete the pairs before the timer runs out.

GAME 2: This version of the game is played with a partner. Place all Problem and Answer Cards face down on the table. Taking turns, each player attempts to match a Problem Card with an Answer Card. The winner is the player with the most matched pairs.

Napier's Bones

Practicing multiplication facts using Napier's Bones

NAME _____

Background Information: Napier's Bones is a fun and effective way for students to practice multiplication facts. The bones are actually multiplication rods. The "main" bone contains the factors 1-9. The bones list the multiples of one of those nine numbers found on the "main" bone. **Activity:** Have students make their own set of bones using tongue depressors or other appropriate materials. You may want to enlarge the "bones" below so they can be cut out and put on a heavier material. "Bone 2" has been done as an example.

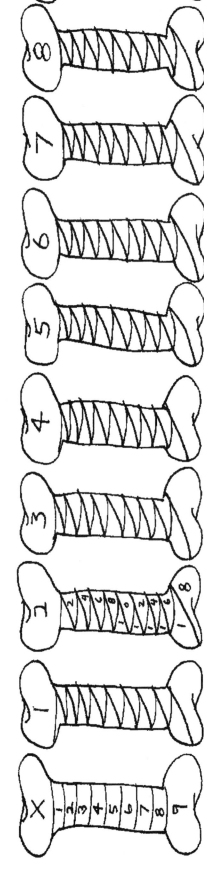

To multiply 4 x 6, use the main bone and the "6" bone:

To divide 64 by 8, use the bones this way:

To multiply more than one digit, study the example below:

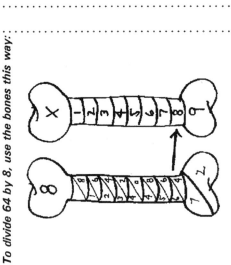

$$754$$
$$\times\ 6$$

$$4 \times 6 = \quad 24$$
$$5 \times 6 = \quad 30$$
$$7 \times 6 = \quad 42$$
$$\overline{4,524}$$

Use your *bones* to practice these multiplication and division problems:

1. $7 \times 8 =$ _____
2. $7 \times 3 =$ _____
3. $6 \times 9 =$ _____
4. $6 \times 6 =$ _____

5. $72 \div 9 =$ _____
6. $63 \div 9 =$ _____
7. $24 \div 6 =$ _____
8. $36 \div 6 =$ _____

9. $73 \times 9 =$ _____
10. $64 \times 6 =$ _____
11. $834 \times 5 =$ _____
12. $367 \times 7 =$ _____

ASTOUNDING NINES

Trick 1

Here are some tricks for learning your 9s.

Trick One - Hold out hands, palms down. Give each finger a number from 1 to 10 starting from the left (example 1).

Example 1   Example 2

Now suppose you want to multiply 9 x 3. Here is how you use your fingers. Tuck under finger 3. What do you observe? You have *two* fingers to the left of the tucked in finger and *seven* fingers to the right. The answer is 9 x 3 = 27 (example 2). Now, you try doing the rest of the 9s. *Pretty astounding!*

Trick Two - Below is a listing of the 9s multiplication facts starting with 9 x 2.
Notice that the product always begins with a digit that is *one less* than the number being multiplied.

Trick 2

9 x 2 = 18
9 x 3 = 27
9 x 4 = 36
9 x 5 = 45
9 x 6 = 54
9 x 7 = 63
9 x 8 = 72

9 x 2 - The product begins with 1 and 1 + _____ = 9. The answer is 8.   So, 9 x 2 = 18.
9 x 3 - The product begins with 2 and 2 + _____ = 9. The answer is 7.   So, 9 x 3 = 27.
Try using this trick to practice your nines facts!!

Trick Three - It's just a matter of adding!

Look carefully at the listing of facts above. Can you see that each product always adds up to 9? For example, 9 x 2 = 18, and 1 + 8 = 9, or 9 x 4 = 36, and 3 + 6 = 9. Another pattern that is *pretty astounding* is if you start with the ones place at the bottom of the facts chart, (9 x 9 = 81) you can discover that the numbers are in order from 1 to 8, *and* if you start with 9 x 2 which is 18 and observe what happens in the ten's place, it too starts with 1 and stays in order from 1 to 9. See how quickly you can write your nines facts using this trick.

Trick 3

NAME_____

Jumbled Number Facts

DIRECTIONS: Rearrange the numbers in
each box to form a multiplication fact.
An example has been done for you.

6	2
4	7

6 x 7 = 42

1.
8	4
6	8

2.
9	2
3	7

3.
4	6
1	4

4.
9	7
8	2

5.
8	1
9	9

6.
7	5
3	5

7.
7	4
9	7

8.
8	6
1	2

9.
5	3
6	0

10.
3	1
2	4

11.
9	7
3	6

12.
4	0
2	5

13.
7	8
6	5

14.
9	4
5	5

15.
3	6
8	1

16.
4	6
2	4

Multiplication Magic Squares

DIRECTIONS: Can you discover the "magic" in each of these squares? To the right is an example.

EXAMPLE:

3 × 2 = 6

3	2	6
1	■	4
3	8	24

3 × 1 = 3 $\frac{× 4}{24}$ 6

3 × 8 = 24

1.

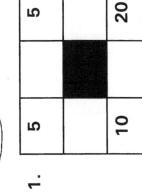

5		5
	■	
20		10

2.

10		5
	■	6
30		

3.

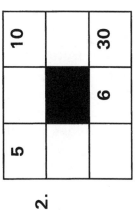

4		2
	■	
20		10

4.

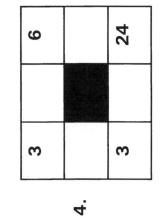

6		3
	■	
24		3

5.

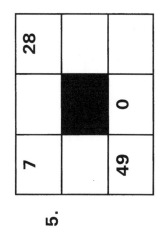

28		7
	■	
	0	49

6.

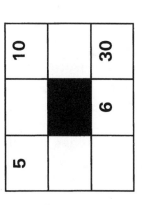

28		7
	■	
	2	14

7.

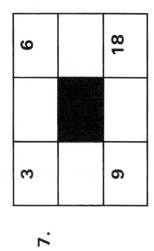

6		3
	■	
18		9

8.

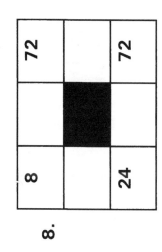

72		8
	■	
72		24

MULTIPLICATION GAMES

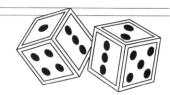

GAME ONE: THE ROLL OF THE DICE. *Objective:* To practice multiplication facts 1-6. *Materials needed:* a pair of dice for every two students along with a copy of the Times Table and the game board "Total Blackout". *Number of players:* 2

Rules: Player One rolls the dice and multiplies the numbers on the dice. If his product is correct (partner can check correctness on the Times Table) he writes the corresponding product in the appropriate box on the "Total Blackout" board. For example, if 6 and 4 were rolled, he would write 24 in the 4th row, 6th column of the grid. If his answer were incorrect, he would lose the opportunity to fill in his grid on that turn and Player Two gets a turn to roll. Both players continue to roll alternating turns. If either player rolls a combination he has rolled previously, he forfeits his turn. The first player to *black out* the entire board is the winner.

Variation: This game can also be played with dominoes. Since there is a zero or blank side for dominoes, it will be necessary to add a zero to the students' grid. All dominoes are turned face down and as with the Blackout game students take turns turning over dominoes and writing the corresponding product in the appropriate box on the grid.

GAME TWO: MULTIPLICATION CARD GAME. *Objective:* To practice multiplication facts 1-10. *Materials needed:* A deck of cards and a Multiplication Facts chart, page 81 in the Appendix. *Number of players:* 2

Directions: Remove the picture cards, aces, and jokers. Students shuffle the remaining cards and divide the deck in half. Each student turns up one card from his/her deck. The first player to call out the correct product gets to keep the cards. However, if the wrong answer is called out, both cards go to the other player. The game continues until all cards have been played. Then, each player shuffles the cards he/she has collected and begins a second round of play. When one player has accumulated all the cards the game is over, and the player is declared "the grand champion." If this process takes too long, a predecided number of rounds can be determined at the beginning of the game, and the player who has the most cards accumulated at the end of the predetermined rounds is the grand champion.

TOTAL BLACKOUT

Grid 1

TOTAL BLACKOUT Grid 2

What do you find twice in "everyday", four times in "every week", and once in a "year"?

EXAMPLE:	(6 x 6) + (6 x 2) + (8 x 3) =
	36 + 12 + 24 = 72

DIRECTIONS: Solve each problem and find your answer in the decoder. Each time your answer appears in the decoder, write the letter of the problem above it. An example has been done for you.

1. (6 x 6) + (6 x 3) + (8 x 3) =
    _____ + _____ + _____ = _____ (F)

2. (7 x 8) + (7 x 9) + (3 x 5) =
    _____ + _____ + _____ = _____ (D)

3. (2 x 1) + (9 x 7) + (5 x 8) =
    _____ + _____ + _____ = _____ (H)

4. (10 x 9) + (7 x 4) + (3 x 1) =
    _____ + _____ + _____ = _____ (N)

5. (6 x 9) + (11 x 4) + (7 x 7) =
    _____ + _____ + _____ = _____ (O)

6. (5 x 20) + (3 x 12) =
    _____ + _____ = _____ (T)

7. (7 x 12) + (6 x 3) + (4 x 5) =
    _____ + _____ + _____ = _____ (Y)

8. (6 x 7) + (4 x 8) + (3 x 9) =
    _____ + _____ + _____ = _____ (R)

9. (8 x 30) + (7 x 8) =
    _____ + _____ = _____ (U)

10. (0 x 3) + (8 x 6) + (3 x 2) =
    _____ + _____ + _____ = _____ (I)

11. (4 x 22) + (6 x 12) =
    _____ + _____ = _____ (L)

12. (9 x 0) + (7 x 3) =
    _____ + _____ = _____ (E)

122	147	296		78	54	121	134		136	105	21

	160	21	136	136	21	101		21

NAME _____

Multiplying one-digit factors by two- and three-digit factors

What do baby birds eat for dessert?

DIRECTIONS: Solve each problem and find your answer in the decoder. Each time you find your answer, write the letter of the problem above it. You may find it easier to work these problems using graph paper. *See example.*

$$356 \times 7 = 2{,}492$$

	3	5	6
3		x	7
4	2	4	2
	2		

1. $34 \times 7 =$ _____ (T)

2. $652 \times 4 =$ _____ (A)

3. $50 \times 2 =$ _____ (E)

4. $357 \times 3 =$ _____ (K)

5. $241 \times 6 =$ _____ (H)

6. $15 \times 7 =$ _____ (P)

7. $770 \times 9 =$ _____ (S)

8. $57 \times 5 =$ _____ (I)

9. $398 \times 1 =$ _____ (R)

10. $82 \times 5 =$ _____ (L)

11. $800 \times 2 =$ _____ (C)

12. $614 \times 8 =$ _____ (O)

___ ___ ___ ___ ___ ___ ___ ___
1,600 1,446 285 1,446 398 4,912 105 1,600

___ ___ ___ ___ ___ ___ ___
1,600 4,912 410 4,912 2,608 4,912 1,071

___ ___ ___ ___ ___
238 285 100 4,912 6,930 100

Why do frogs have it made?

DIRECTIONS: Solve each problem below and find your
answer in the decoder. Each time your answer appears in
the decoder, write the letter of the problem above it.

		3	1	4
	x		6	3
	1	9	4	2
1	8	8	4	0
1	9	7	8	2

$$314 \times 63 = 19{,}782$$

TIP: You may find it easier to work longer multiplication
problems using graph paper. *See example.*

1.   57 x 36 = _____ (Y)

2.   531 x 21 = _____ (T)

3.   62 x 40 = _____ (A)   8.   759 x 67 = _____(U)

4.   99 x 18 = _____ (H)   9.   74 x 62 = _____ (G)

5.   597 x 76 = _____ (M)   10.   298 x 42 = _____ (W)

6.   95 x 43 = _____ (S)   11.   67 x 56 = _____ (B)

7.   81 x 74 = _____ (E)

_____ _____ _____ _____
11,151   1,782   5,994   2,052

        _____ _____ _____
        5,994   2,480   11,151

_____ _____ _____ _____
12,516   1,782   2,480   11,151

_____ _____ _____ _____
3,752   50,853   4,588   4,085

_____ _____ _____ _____
11,151   1,782   5,994   45,372

Using window or lattice multiplication

NAME

Multiplication Made Easy by Using the Lattice Method

My crystal ball tells me you might like this Lattice Multiplication!

This very old method invented in 1478 A.D. is a fun, fascinating way to practice and check multiplication problems. Study the example below, and then read the directions to see if you can understand how this method works.

Notice in the right square is the product of 5 and 6 which is 30. To its left is the product of 6 x 4 which is 24. And in the last square to the left is the product of 6 x 2 which is 12. The final product is found by adding numbers along the diagonals, starting with the lower right square and regrouping to the next diagonal when necessary. The product of 245 x 6 is 1,470.

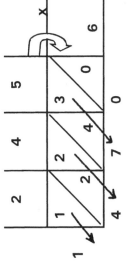

245 x 6 = 1,470

DIRECTIONS: Now, it's your turn to try the "lattice method" to see if it makes multiplication easier for you.

1.

2.

3.

4.

5.

6.

Super Challenge: Make your own lattice boards and solve these problems:
6,783 x 2,346
31,245 x 4,568

If you cross Bambi with a ghost, what would you have?

Name _____

DIRECTIONS: Solve each problem and then find your answer in the decoder. Each time your answer occurs in the decoder, write the letter of the problem above it. Study these examples and see if you can discover the shortcut method for dividing.

```
      1 2 R1          1 3 7 R5        9 4 7 R3
    6)7 ¹3          7)9 ²6 ⁵4       4)37 ¹9 ³1
```

THINK: Each place value must be crossed out as it is used, and the remainder is written beside the next place value.

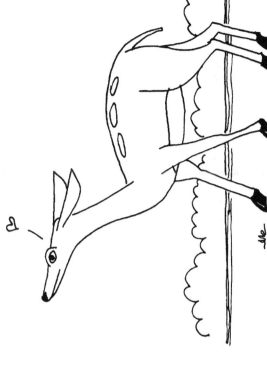

1. 3)8 4 5 = H

6. 6)3, 6 5 2 = O

2. 7)9, 4 8 6 = E

7. 3)9, 4 8 6 = A

3. 8)1, 0 4 6 = D

8. 9)1 0, 6 5 3 = Y

4. 5)7, 8 4 3 = U

9. 7)$6 4. 3 3 = M

5. 2)8 0 9 = V

10. 8)4, 0 0 1 = B

1,183 R6	608 R4	1,568 R3	130 R6	3,162	$9.19	500 R1	281 R2	3,162	404 R1	1,355 R1
		500 R1	3,162			500 R1	608 R4	608 R4		

NAME _____

What's the definition of a flood?

DIRECTIONS: First, solve each problem below on another sheet of paper. **Second,** find your answer in the decoder at the bottom of the page. **Third,** each time your answer appears in the decoder, write the letter of the problem above it.

EXAMPLE: 576 ÷ 8 = _____

```
         7  2
     8 | 5  7  6
        -5  6    →
         1  6
         1  6
```

You may want to solve these problems using graph paper and the code : <u>D</u>addy, <u>M</u>ommy, <u>S</u>ister, <u>B</u>rother or <u>D</u>ivide, <u>M</u>ultiply, <u>S</u>ubtract, <u>B</u>ring down. An example has been done for you.

1. 396 ÷ 4 = _____ (S)

2. 84 ÷ 3 = _____ (F)

3. 4,146 ÷ 6 = _____ (I)

4. 7,528 ÷ 8 = _____ (H)

5. 294 ÷ 6 = _____ (V)

6. 475 ÷ 5 = _____ (D)

7. 679 ÷ 7 = _____ (T)

8. 747 ÷ 3 = _____ (O)

9. 196 ÷ 2 = _____ (E)

10. 2,755 ÷ 5 = _____ (A)

11. 3,438 ÷ 9 = _____ (B)

12. 238 ÷ 7 = _____ (G)

13. 150 ÷ 10 = _____ (R)

___ ___ ___ ___ ___ ___ ___ , ___ ___ ___ ___ ___ ___ ___ ___
551 15   97 691 97 99   15   99   98   49   691 382 382 691   34

___ ___ ___ ___ ___ ___ ___ ___ ___ ___ ___ ___
97   941 551 97   97   99   249 249 15   95   34   98

___ ___ ___ ___ ___
28   249 691 382 15   99

NAME _____

How far do cows go through school?

Dividing by two-digit divisors

DIRECTIONS: **First**, solve each problem below on another sheet of paper. **Second**, find your answer in the decoder at the bottom of the page. **Third**, each time your answer appears in the decoder, write the letter of the problem above it.

EXAMPLE: 7,812 ÷ 63 = _____

6 3	7 8 1 2		1 2 4
	- 6 3	→	8 1 2
	1 5 1	→	1 5 1
	- 1 2 6	→	2 5 2
	2 5 2		
	- 2 5 2		

TIP: You may want to solve these problems using graph paper and the code: *Daddy, Mommy, Sister, Brother,* or *Divide, Multiply, Subtract, Bring down.* An example has been done for you.

1. 4,256 ÷ 76 = _____ (O)

2. 1,989 ÷ 51 = _____ (R)

3. 384 ÷ 12 = _____ (U)

4. 806 ÷ 13 = _____ (D)

5. 4,268 ÷ 44 = _____ (H)

6. 1,275 ÷ 15 = _____ (L)

7. 156 ÷ 12 = _____ (T)

8. 840 ÷ 35 = _____ (G)

9. 559 ÷ 13 = _____ (E)

10. 847 ÷ 77 = _____ (W)

11. 7,800 ÷ 50 = _____ (C)

13	97	39	56	32	24	97

156	56	11	85	43	62	24	43

NAME _____

What is a dark horse?

DIRECTIONS: First, solve each problem. Second, find your answer in the decoder at the bottom of the page. Third, each time the answer occurs in the decoder, write the letter of the problem above it.

STRATEGY: Add the numbers and divide by how many numbers there are. *For example:* John earned extra money by pet sitting. The amounts earned for six weeks were: $25.50, $30.00, $28.50, $35.50, $28.20 and $29.30. What was John's weekly average for the 6 weeks he worked?

$25.50
30.00
28.50
35.50
28.20
+ 29.30
Step 1 $177.00 ← Total

Step 2
$177.00 ÷ 6 = $29.50

John's average for the six weeks is $29.50

---

1. Kacie was the highest scorer on her soccer team. For her spring season, she scored 4, 3, 3, 4, 5, 4, 4, 4, and 5 goals. What was her average number of goals scored each game?
   _____ = I

2. Derrick's batting averages for 6 months of baseball games is given below listed by each monthly average: .344, .260, .450, .375, .490, and .673. What was his monthly average?
   _____ = H

3. Kelsey's gymnastic vault scores for her 10 meets were: 9.5, 9.3, 8.75, 10.0, 9.25, 9.5, 9.15, 8.90, 9.35, and 9.9. What was her average vaulting score? _____ = A

4. Nishi read 6 books in two weeks. The first book she read had 335 pages, the 2nd book had 340 pages, the 3rd book had 507 pages, the 4th book had 280 pages, the 5th book had 426 pages, and the 6th book had 380 pages. How many pages did Nishi average reading each day? _____ = E

5. Ashleigh earned babysitting money for seven weeks in the summer. She earned $23.50, $31.50, $20.00, $25.00, $32.50, $24.00, and $25.50. What was her weekly average for the seven weeks? _____ = R

6. John wanted to know his average in math. His teacher shared these grades with him: 93, 88, 97, 100, 87, 95, 100, and 92. What was John's math average? _____ = G

7. Kevin was concerned that his 2 zeros for not turning in two Social Studies assignments would greatly affect his average for the 6 weeks. His grades were 100, 87, 78, 0, 95, 0, 89, 90, and 91. What was Kevin's average? _____ = T
   Do you think the two zeros made a big difference in Kevin's grades? Yes _____ No _____

8. David's football team plays 8 games in a season. Last season they scored 9, 17, 21, 7, 18, 28, 13, and 31 points. What was the average number of points scored per game?
   _____ = M

9. Brenna trained for the *Peachtree Road Race* by jogging every day for 45 days. She ran a total of 675 miles. What was the average number of miles Brenna ran each day? _____ = N

___	___	___	___	___	___	___	___	___	___
9.36	15	4	94	.432	70	18	9.36	$26	162

DIRECTIONS: Each of the number recipes below contain a bit of number magic. See if you can discover the magic, and then with the help of your calculator try these potions on a friend.

MAGIC POTIONS

Potion Number One

	EXAMPLE 1	EXAMPLE 2
1. Choose any number.	14	10
2. Multiply by 5.	14 × 5 = 70	10 × 5 = 50
3. Add 6 to the product.	70 + 6 = 76	50 + 6 = 56
4. Multiply the sum by 4.	76 × 4 = 304	56 × 4 = 224
5., Add 9 to the product.	304 + 9 = 313	224 + 9 = 233
6. Multiply the sum by 5.	313 × 5 = 1,565	233 × 5 = 1,165
7. Cross off the last 2 digits.	1,5~~65~~	1,1~~65~~

Potion Number Two

Do you have friends who won't tell you their age? Well, here's a way of finding out. **First,** ask your friend to secretly **multiply her age by three. Second,** have her then **add 6 to** her answer. **Third,** she must **divide the sum by 3** and tell you her answer. **Fourth,** you secretly **subtract 2** from her answer. **The result will always be your friend's true age.**

> This process is done in secret by your friend.
> *Age: 11*
> 1. 11 × 3 = 33
> 2. 33 + 6 = 39
> 3. 39 ÷ 3 = 13
> 4. 13 − 2 = 11
> (Your friend's age)

*Can you figure out why **this** potion always works?*

Potion Number Three

1. Pick any number: 312
2. Multiply by 9: 312 × 9 = 2,808
3. Add the numbers in the product:
   2 + 8 + 0 + 8 = 18
4. The sum of the numbers can always be divided by 9 with no remainder.
   18 ÷ 9 = 2

Potion Number Four

1. Write the year of the your birth: 1989
2. Multiply the year of your birth by 2:
   1989 × 2 = 3,978
3. Add 5: 3,978 + 5 = 3,983
4. Multiply by 50: 3,983 × 50 = 199,150
5. Add your age: 199,150 + 10 = 199,160
6. Add 365: 199,160 + 365 = 199,525
7. Subtract 615: 199,525 − 615 = 198,910

The **first 4 digits** will always be the same as the **year** in which you were **born.** The **last two digits** will always be **your age.** Try this trick on a friend!

NAME _____

Problem Solving Checklist

1. UNDERSTANDING THE PROBLEM
It's important to:
❑ Read the problem carefully.
❑ Look for the important information.
❑ Jot down that information in your own words.
❑ Decide on the key math phrases such as difference, total, etc.

2. SOLVING THE PROBLEM
Think of strategies to try such as one or more of these:
❑ Use manipulatives.
❑ Act it out.
❑ Look for a pattern.
❑ Draw a diagram or picture.
❑ Use calculators or computers.
❑ Guess and check.
❑ Tell and print a story.
❑ Make an organized list or table.
❑ Simplify the problem by using smaller numbers.
❑ Write an equation.
❑ Work backwards.
❑ Use reasoning (logical thinking).

3. CHECKING THE PROBLEM
❑ Did you use all of the important information?
❑ Did you check your calculations?
❑ Does your answer make sense?
❑ Can you explain to someone else how you solved the problem?

Solving story problems using whole number operations

Why did Dracula go to the orthodontist?

DIRECTIONS: Solve each of the problems and then find your answer in the decoder. Each time your answers appears in the decoder, write the letter of the problem above it.

1. If a hummingbird can flap its wings up to 70 times per second, how many times can it flap its wings in a minute? _____ = **S**

2. Do you believe a cricket can give you the exact temperature in Fahrenheit degrees? It can. You count the number of chirps in 14 seconds and then add 40. So, if a cricket chirped 42 times in 14 seconds, what would the temperature be? _____ = **O**

3. A white rhinoceros can weigh up to 3½ tons. How many pounds are in 3½ tons? _____ = **R**

4. On the German Autobahn where there is no speed limit, if a car traveled 300 miles in 2 hours, how many miles did it average per hour? _____ = **M**

5. You shed your skin continually and replace it with an entirely new outer layer every 28 days. How many times would you have shed your skin in 252 days? _____ = **T**

6. The pouch of a pelican can stretch so much that it can carry 12 quarts of water or 30 pounds of fish. How many gallons of water can it carry? _____ = **H**

7. If your heart beats about 70 times per minute, about how many times does it beat in 3 hours? _____ = **I**

8. Did you know the amount of blood in your body depends on how big you are? For example, if you weigh about 32 lbs., you would have about 1 quart of blood in your body. About how much would you weigh if you had about 3 quarts of blood in your body? _____ = **E**

9. In each beehive there are approximately 75,000 bees. There is only 1 queen bee and she can lay an average of 2,000 eggs per day. At that rate how many eggs could she lay in a year? _____ = **V**

10. It takes the nectar from 2,000 flowers to make one tablespoon of honey. How many tablespoons of honey can be made from the nectar of 10,000 flowers? _____ = **B**

11. An elephant can weigh up to 14,000 pounds, but its brain only weighs approximately 11 pounds. How much of the elephant's weight is not in its brain? _____ = **P**

| 9 | 82 | | 12,600 | 150 | 13,989 | 7,000 | 82 | 730,000 | 96 |

| 3 | 12,600 | 4,200 | | 5 | 12,600 | 9 | 96 |

©2000 by Incentive Publications, Inc., Nashville, TN.

NAME _____

ROCKET BOOSTERS

DIRECTIONS: Fill in each stage of the rocket with a pair of factors for the composite number in the cone of each rocket. The first one is done for you.

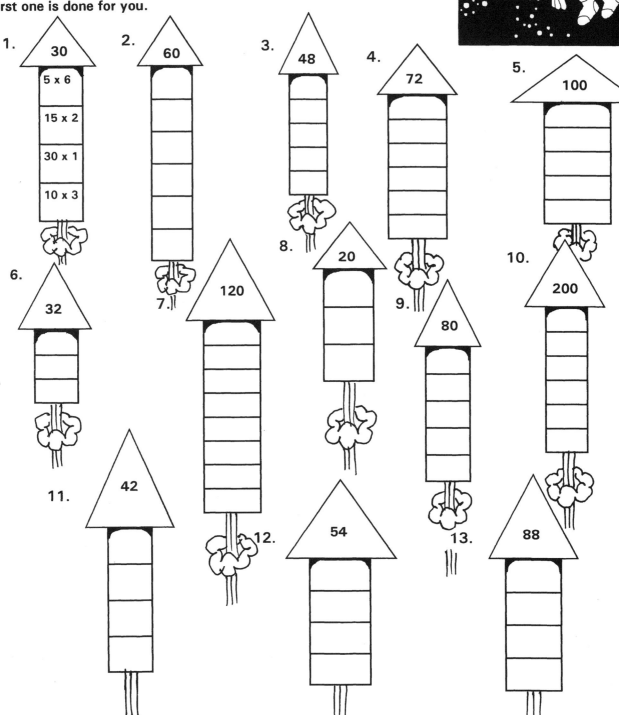

1. **30**
5 x 6
15 x 2
30 x 1
10 x 3

2. **60**

3. **48**

4. **72**

5. **100**

6. **32**

7. **120**

8. **20**

9. **80**

10. **200**

11. **42**

12. **54**

13. **88**

Here's a challenge for you! Draw 3-5 rocket boosters and ask a friend to find the correct factors.

PRIME OR COMPOSITE?

A **prime number** is a whole number *greater than one* that has exactly two factors, 1 and itself.

A **composite number** is a whole number *greater than one* that has more than two factors.

DIRECTIONS: Complete the table below. If the number is a composite, you will need to give only one set of factors to prove that the number is a composite. (*For example*, if the number is 36, you can give 12 and 3, 2 and 18, 6 and 6, or 4 and 9.) The first and second ones have been done for you. Use the Table of Factors found in the Appendix to help you.

	Number	**One Set of Factors**	**Prime or Composite**
1.	20	5, 4	Composite
2.	17	1, 17	Prime
3.	33		
4.	36		
5.	11		
6.	15		
7.	29		
8.	13		
9.	112		
10.	47		
11.	87		
12.	99		
13.	83		
14.	48		
15.	93		
16.	57		
17.	49		
18.	100		
19.	41		
20.	71		

Clue: You should have **8 primes** and **12 composites** including the 2 examples.

PRIME FACTOR BUBBLE MAGIC

DIRECTIONS: To find the prime factors of the composite number shown in the top of each bubble, fill in the adjoining bubbles with factors of the composite number. There may be several combinations that will work but your choice of combinations depends on the number of bubbles available. Under each set of bubbles, write an equation proving that you have identified the correct prime factors. The first one has been done for you.

1.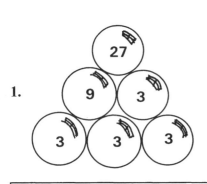

$$(3 \times 3) \times 3 =$$
$$9 \times 3 = 27$$

2.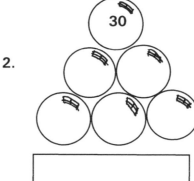

3.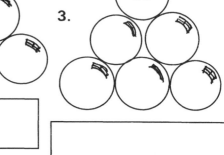

4.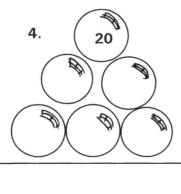

5.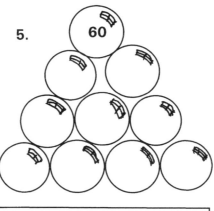

6.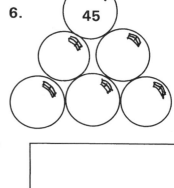

7.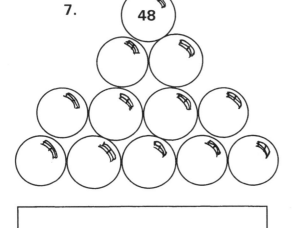

8.

Using the slide method to find the GCF, LCM, and fraction in lowest terms

NAME _____

The Slide Works!!

Wow! This "Slide" really makes fractions easier.

DIRECTIONS: Examine the method shown below for finding the *greatest common factor, least common multiple,* and the *fraction in lowest terms of 24 and 36.*

```
any common factor-  6 | 24   36
any common factor-  2 |  4    6
                         2    3
```

(1) To find the *GCF*, multiply the numbers outside the steps on the slide on the left side of the table: (6 x 2 = 12). 12 is the GCF. (2) To find the *LCM*, multiply all of the numbers outside of the slide's border: (6 x 2 x 2 x 3 = 72). 72 is the LCM. (3) The fraction in lowest terms is shown by the two numbers underneath the slide. Therefore, the fraction is $\frac{2}{3}$ in lowest terms. Now, you try using the slide to find the *GCF, LCM,* and *fraction in lowest terms* of the composite numbers shown in the chart.

	GCF	LCM	Lowest terms
1. 6, 12			
2. 18, 24			
3. 10, 15			
4. 12, 16			
5. 18, 34			
6. 9, 12			
7. 20, 30			
8. 18, 36			

	GCF	LCM	Lowest terms
9. 25, 70			
10. 22, 44			
11. 17, 34			
12. 18, 48			
13. 24, 60			
14. 29, 40			
15. 25, 100			
16. 15, 60			

MAKING FRACTION KITS – Part One

MATERIALS NEEDED: A Fraction Kit for each student consisting of: 5 different colored 3" x 18" construction paper strips, scissors, pencil or colored marker, and one unmarked cube labeled as follows:

$$\frac{1}{2}, \frac{1}{4}, \frac{1}{8}, \frac{2}{8}, \frac{1}{16}, \frac{2}{16}$$

DIRECTIONS FOR MAKING KITS: ❶ Students are given a legal size envelope with the 5 strips of colored construction paper and the one die that has been labeled. They are directed to remove the strips from the envelope and place them on a flat surface. Talk about the fact that the strips each represent "1 WHOLE." Label one strip "1 Whole."

1 Whole

❷ Fold a 2nd strip into halves. Ask students how many sections they will have when they open their folded strip. Ask them to label each part $\frac{1}{2}$ and cut the strip on the folded line and place on the whole.

$\frac{1}{2}$	$\frac{1}{2}$

❸ Take another strip and fold in half two times. Ask students how many sections they will have when the strip is unfolded. Label each part $\frac{1}{4}$ and cut them apart and place on the whole.

$\frac{1}{4}$	$\frac{1}{4}$	$\frac{1}{4}$	$\frac{1}{4}$

❹ Take another strip and fold it in half three times. Ask students how many sections they will have when the strip is unfolded. Label each part $\frac{1}{8}$ and cut them apart and place on the whole.

$\frac{1}{8}$	$\frac{1}{8}$	$\frac{1}{8}$	$\frac{1}{8}$	$\frac{1}{8}$	$\frac{1}{8}$	$\frac{1}{8}$	$\frac{1}{8}$

❺ Take the last strip and fold it in half four times. Again, ask students how many sections they will have when the strip is unfolded. Label each part $\frac{1}{16}$ and cut them apart carefully and place on the whole.

$\frac{1}{16}$	$\frac{1}{16}$	$\frac{1}{16}$	$\frac{1}{16}$	$\frac{1}{16}$	$\frac{1}{16}$	$\frac{1}{16}$	$\frac{1}{16}$	$\frac{1}{16}$	$\frac{1}{16}$	$\frac{1}{16}$	$\frac{1}{16}$	$\frac{1}{16}$	$\frac{1}{16}$	$\frac{1}{16}$	$\frac{1}{16}$

Advise students to keep their strips in an envelope which has their name on it. They will then be ready to use their kits to play games that will make learning fractions easier and more fun!

LET THE GAMES BEGIN! - Part Two

DIRECTIONS: Use the fraction kit you have created to play these fraction games.

FRACTION KIT GAME ONE
FRACTION COVER UP
Game for 2-4 Players

☐   Put your "1 whole" strip on a flat surface in front of you.

☐   Take turns rolling the die.

☐   Take the fraction part you rolled on the die and place it on your "1 whole". For example, if you roll $\frac{1}{4}$, this fractional piece is laid on the "1 whole".

☐   The first player to cover his/her "1 whole" exactly wins. If your last piece goes over "1 whole" you lose that turn and the next player rolls.

☐   You might want to play the best 2 out of 3, or 3 out of 4 games, or come up with your own combination of how many games will be played in order to determine a winner.

FRACTION KIT GAME TWO
FRACTION EXCHANGE – SUBTRACTION
Game for 2-4 Players

☐   Begin with your "1 whole" covered with two halves.

☐   Take turns rolling the die.

☐   Whatever you roll, you take off, or subtract, from that fraction. You may need to make an exchange first. For example, if you roll $\frac{1}{4}$ on your first roll, you will need to exchange $\frac{1}{2}$ for $\frac{2}{4}$ before you can subtract $\frac{1}{4}$.

☐   The winner is the first player to uncover his "1 whole" exactly.

More Ideas

☐   Play to see who can have the largest number after four turns.

☐   Put two fraction kits together and play to cover the "2 wholes" exactly. This same procedure can work for subtracting, as is explained in Fraction Kit Game Two.

Adding and subtracting like fractions with no regrouping

DIRECTIONS: Solve each problem and then find your answer in the decoder. Each time your answer appears in the decoder, write the letter of the problem above it.

How is life like a shower?

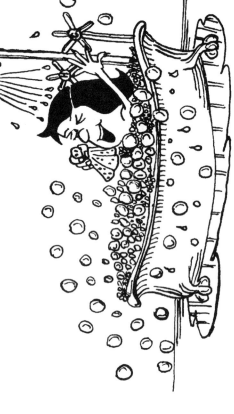

1. $\frac{7}{10} + \frac{2}{10} =$ _____ (A)

2. $\frac{1}{4} + \frac{2}{4} =$ _____ (Y)

3. $\frac{7}{8} - \frac{4}{8} =$ _____ (E)

4. $\frac{3}{7} - \frac{1}{7} =$ _____ (U)

5. $\frac{5}{8} + \frac{2}{8} =$ _____ (N)

6. $\frac{27}{38} - \frac{10}{38} =$ _____ (R)

7. $\frac{19}{20} - \frac{10}{20} =$ _____ (D)

8. $\frac{6}{7} - \frac{3}{7} =$ _____ (I)

9. $\frac{15}{28} + \frac{4}{28} =$ _____ (T)

10. $\frac{10}{20} + \frac{7}{20} =$ _____ (O)

11. $\frac{13}{28} - \frac{2}{28} =$ _____ (W)

12. $\frac{3}{10} + \frac{4}{10} =$ _____ (G)

13. $\frac{3}{8} + \frac{2}{8} =$ _____ (H)

Decoder:

$\frac{3}{4}$ $\frac{17}{20}$ $\frac{7}{8}$ $\frac{2}{7}$ $\frac{3}{8}$ $\frac{11}{28}$ $\frac{17}{38}$ $\frac{3}{8}$, $\frac{17}{20}$ $\frac{17}{38}$ $\frac{7}{8}$ $\frac{7}{10}$ $\frac{19}{28}$ $\frac{17}{20}$ $\frac{2}{7}$ $\frac{7}{8}$ $\frac{17}{38}$ $\frac{19}{28}$ $\frac{5}{8}$ $\frac{9}{10}$ $\frac{7}{8}$ $\frac{11}{28}$ $\frac{9}{10}$ $\frac{19}{28}$ $\frac{3}{8}$ $\frac{7}{8}$ $\frac{9}{20}$ $\frac{3}{8}$ $\frac{17}{38}$

NAME _____

What do bakers use as the main ingredient in dog biscuits?

DIRECTIONS: Reduce each fraction to lowest terms and find your answer in the decoder. Each time your answer appears in the decoder, write the letter of the problem above it. An example has been done for you.

$$\frac{6}{8} \div \frac{2}{2} = \frac{3}{4}$$

1. $\frac{20}{36} =$ _____ (R)

2. $\frac{4}{14} =$ _____ (I)

3. $\frac{15}{20} =$ _____ (E)

4. $\frac{10}{12} =$ _____ (U)

5. $\frac{20}{40} =$ _____ (H)

6. $\frac{9}{27} =$ _____ (S)

7. $\frac{14}{26} =$ _____ (Y)

8. $\frac{15}{25} =$ _____ (O)

9. $\frac{4}{36} =$ _____ (L)

10. $\frac{11}{66} =$ _____ (F)

11. $\frac{12}{18} =$ _____ (T)

12. $\frac{21}{30} =$ _____ (C)

_____ _____ _____ _____ _____ _____ _____ _____ _____ _____
$\frac{2}{3}$ $\frac{1}{2}$ $\frac{1}{9}$ $\frac{3}{4}$ $\frac{7}{13}$ $\frac{5}{6}$ $\frac{1}{3}$ $\frac{3}{4}$ $\frac{5}{6}$ $\frac{5}{9}$

_____ _____ _____ _____ _____ _____ _____ _____ _____
$\frac{3}{5}$ $\frac{1}{9}$ $\frac{2}{7}$ $\frac{1}{9}$ $\frac{1}{6}$ $\frac{1}{3}$ $\frac{3}{5}$ $\frac{3}{5}$ $\frac{5}{6}$

_____ _____ _____
$\frac{7}{10}$ $\frac{3}{5}$ $\frac{5}{9}$

Changing fractions to mixed numbers

NAME _____

What's a band director's favorite day of the year?

DIRECTIONS: Change each fraction to a whole or mixed number in lowest terms. Find your answer in the decoder. Each time your answer appears in the decoder, write the letter of the problem above it.

Example: $\frac{5}{3} = 5 \div 3 = 1\frac{2}{3}$

1. $\frac{7}{4} =$ _____ (I)

2. $\frac{15}{10} =$ _____ (A)

3. $\frac{8}{4} =$ _____ (O)

4. $\frac{40}{12} =$ _____ (T)

5. $\frac{14}{11} =$ _____ (R)

6. $\frac{22}{16} =$ _____ (F)

7. $\frac{9}{3} =$ _____ (U)

8. $\frac{21}{5} =$ _____ (H)

9. $\frac{36}{8} =$ _____ (M)

10. $\frac{25}{10} =$ _____ (C)

11. $\frac{8}{6} =$ _____ (S)

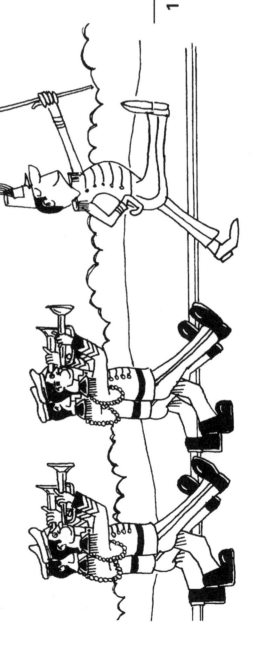

$\overline{1\frac{3}{8}}$ $\overline{4\frac{1}{2}}$ $\overline{2}$ $\overline{3}$ $\overline{1\frac{3}{11}}$ $\overline{3\frac{1}{3}}$ $\overline{1\frac{1}{3}}$

$\overline{1\frac{3}{4}}$ $\overline{4\frac{1}{2}}$ $\overline{1\frac{1}{2}}$ $\overline{1\frac{3}{11}}$ $\overline{2\frac{1}{2}}$ $\overline{4\frac{1}{5}}$,

$\overline{1\frac{3}{11}}$ $\overline{3\frac{1}{3}}$ $\overline{4\frac{1}{5}}$

NAME _____

Changing mixed numbers to fractions

What's the definition of an igloo?

DIRECTIONS: Change each mixed number to a fraction and then find your answer in the decoder. Each time your answer appears in the decoder, write the letter of the problem above it.

$3\frac{3}{8} = 3$ wholes which can be written as $\frac{24}{8}$ and then add $\frac{3}{8}$ more and you'll have $\frac{27}{8}$, *OR* 1 whole $= \frac{8}{8}$, 2 wholes $= \frac{16}{8}$, 3 wholes $= \frac{24}{8}$, and then add $\frac{3}{8}$ more and the total will be $\frac{27}{8}$.

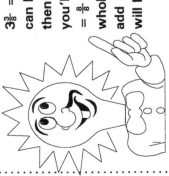

1. $4\frac{2}{5} =$ _____ (A)

2. $8\frac{1}{2} =$ _____ (O)

3. $10\frac{1}{3} =$ _____ (B)

4. $2\frac{2}{3} =$ _____ (T)

5. $3\frac{3}{4} =$ _____ (L)

6. $7\frac{3}{5} =$ _____ (U)

7. $5\frac{5}{6} =$ _____ (E)

8. $3\frac{2}{3} =$ _____ (R)

9. $1\frac{5}{6} =$ _____ (W)

10. $6\frac{3}{4} =$ _____ (N)

11. $2\frac{3}{7} =$ _____ (I)

12. $4\frac{2}{11} =$ _____ (C)

13. $1\frac{1}{5} =$ _____ (F)

Decoder:

$\dfrac{17}{2}$ $\dfrac{11}{6}$ $\dfrac{8}{3}$

$\dfrac{35}{6}$ $\dfrac{11}{3}$

$\dfrac{15}{4}$ $\dfrac{17}{2}$ $\dfrac{6}{5}$

$\dfrac{46}{11}$ $\dfrac{17}{7}$ $\dfrac{46}{11}$ $\dfrac{8}{3}$

$\dfrac{17}{7}$ $\dfrac{27}{4}$ $\dfrac{22}{5}$ $\dfrac{38}{5}$ $\dfrac{17}{7}$ $\dfrac{15}{4}$ $\dfrac{38}{5}$ $\dfrac{31}{3}$

NAME _____

What did the Martians say when they landed on Earth by mistake?

DIRECTIONS: Solve each problem below and then find your answer in the decoder. Each time your answer appears in the decoder, write the letter of the problem above it. Many of your fractional answers will need to be reduced to lowest terms.

1. $\frac{1}{2} \times \frac{2}{3} =$ _____ (S)

2. $\frac{3}{8} \times \frac{2}{5} =$ _____ (N)

3. $\frac{3}{4} \times \frac{2}{9} =$ _____ (A)

4. $\frac{2}{7} \times \frac{1}{6} =$ _____ (R)

5. $\frac{3}{8} \times \frac{5}{12} =$ _____ (D)

6. $\frac{1}{2} \times \frac{1}{2} =$ _____ (Y)

7. $\frac{3}{8} \times \frac{3}{10} =$ _____ (T)

8. $\frac{5}{11} \times \frac{11}{12} =$ _____ (L)

9. $\frac{2}{3} \times \frac{3}{4} =$ _____ (W)

10. $\frac{3}{5} \times \frac{2}{5} =$ _____ (H)

11. $\frac{3}{4} \times \frac{1}{2} =$ _____ (P)

12. $\frac{1}{3} \times \frac{1}{3} =$ _____ (E)

13. $\frac{5}{9} \times \frac{3}{7} =$ _____ (O)

14. $\frac{7}{8} \times \frac{4}{5} =$ _____ (I)

____ ____ ____ ____ ____   ____ ____ ,
$\frac{1}{3}$ $\frac{5}{21}$ $\frac{1}{21}$ $\frac{1}{21}$ $\frac{1}{4}$ $\frac{1}{2}$ $\frac{1}{9}$

'

____ ____ ____ ____ ____
$\frac{5}{32}$ $\frac{7}{10}$ $\frac{5}{32}$ $\frac{3}{20}$ $\frac{9}{80}$

____ ____ ____ ____ ____ ____
$\frac{3}{8}$ $\frac{5}{12}$ $\frac{1}{6}$ $\frac{3}{20}$ $\frac{1}{9}$ $\frac{9}{80}$

____ ____ ____ ____   ____ ____ ____
$\frac{9}{80}$ $\frac{6}{25}$ $\frac{7}{10}$ $\frac{1}{3}$ $\frac{1}{2}$ $\frac{1}{6}$ $\frac{1}{4}$

NAME_____

What continent do you see the first thing in the morning?

DIRECTIONS: Solve each problem and then find your answer in the decoder. Each time your answer appears in the decoder, write the answer of the problem above it.

Example:

1. $2\frac{2}{3} \times 3\frac{3}{4} =$ 2 5 2. $\frac{8}{3} \times \frac{15}{4} =$ Or 3. $\frac{2}{1} \times \frac{5}{1} = 10$	1. $2\frac{2}{3} \times 3\frac{3}{4} =$ 2. $\frac{8}{3} \times \frac{15}{4} =$ 3. 8 x 15 (numerators multiplied) = 120 4. 3 x 4 (denominators multiplied) = 12 5. $\frac{120}{12} = 120 \div 12 = 10$

1. $2\frac{2}{3} \times 2\frac{3}{4} =$ _____ (R)

2. $1\frac{1}{3} \times 7 =$ _____ (S)

3. $6\frac{2}{5} \times 8\frac{3}{4} =$ _____ (P)

4. $1\frac{1}{2} \times 3\frac{3}{5} =$ _____ (U)

5. $1\frac{5}{6} \times 3 =$ _____ (O)

6. $2\frac{7}{9} \times 6\frac{3}{5} =$ _____ (Y)

7. $8 \times \frac{2}{3} =$ _____ (E)

$\overline{}$ $\overline{}$ $\overline{}$ $\overline{}$ $\overline{}$ $\overline{}$ $\overline{}$ $\overline{}$ $\overline{}$ $\overline{}$ $\overline{}$ $\overline{}$

$18\frac{1}{3}$ $5\frac{1}{2}$ $5\frac{2}{5}$ $9\frac{1}{3}$ $5\frac{1}{3}$ $5\frac{1}{3}$ $5\frac{1}{3}$ $5\frac{2}{5}$ $7\frac{1}{3}$ $5\frac{1}{2}$ 56 $5\frac{1}{3}$

NAME_____

What did the man say when he became the father of triplets?

DIRECTIONS: Solve each problem below and locate your answer in the decoder. Each time the answer appears in the decoder, write the letter of the problem above it. An example and some helpful hints are given below.

Example: $\frac{1}{2} \div \frac{1}{4} =$

Think: How many $\frac{1}{4}$s can be made from $\frac{1}{2}$?

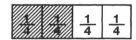

If $\frac{1}{2}$ were divided into $\frac{1}{4}$s, how many $\frac{1}{4}$s would there be? Use this diagram to help you answer this question.

There are two $\frac{1}{4}$s in $\frac{1}{2}$; therefore $\frac{1}{2} \div \frac{1}{4} = 2$. See if this technique can help you in solving these problems. You may want to draw your own diagrams to help you understand how to divide simple fractions.

1. $2 \div \frac{1}{3} =$ _____ (T)

2. $3 \div \frac{1}{3} =$ _____ (I)

3. $\frac{1}{2} \div \frac{1}{8} =$ _____ (V)

4. $3 \div \frac{1}{5} =$ _____ (C)

5. $4 \div \frac{1}{4} =$ _____ (E)

6. $\frac{3}{4} \div \frac{3}{4} =$ _____ (N)

7. $4 \div \frac{1}{3} =$ _____ (M)

8. $1 \div \frac{1}{2} =$ _____ (Y)

9. $8 \div \frac{1}{3} =$ _____ (B)

10. $7 \div \frac{1}{2} =$ _____ (L)

11. $3 \div \frac{1}{6} =$ _____ (U)

12. $\frac{1}{3} \div \frac{1}{9} =$ _____ (A)

13. $4 \div \frac{1}{2} =$ _____ (S)

,

| 9 | 15 | 3 | 1 | 6 | 24 | 16 | 14 | 9 | 16 | 4 | 16 |

| 12 | 2 | 15 | 16 | 1 | 8 | 18 | 8 |

AND THE WINNER IS...

DIRECTIONS: Solve each problem below and then circle your answer on one of the cards below. Three answers in a row make a winning card.

STRATEGIES : $2\frac{3}{4} \div 3\frac{3}{8} =$

Step 1: Change mixed numbers to fractions: $\frac{11}{4} \div \frac{27}{8} =$

Step 2 : Invert the second fraction and change ÷ to x: $\frac{11}{4} \times \frac{8}{27}$

Step 3 : Multiply numerators and then denominators: $\frac{11}{4} \times \frac{8}{27} =$

Step 4 : Reduce product to its lowest terms: $\frac{88}{108} \div \frac{4}{4} = \frac{22}{27}$

1. $1\frac{1}{2} \div \frac{2}{3} =$ _____

2. $6\frac{1}{3} \div 4\frac{1}{6} =$ _____

3. $10\frac{1}{2} \div 1\frac{1}{2} =$ ____

4. $5\frac{1}{4} \div 1\frac{1}{2} =$ _____

5. $20 \div 1\frac{1}{4} =$ _____

6. $9 \div 2\frac{1}{4} =$ _____

7. $7 \div 3\frac{1}{2} =$ _____

8. $\frac{5}{9} \div 1\frac{1}{4} =$ _____

9. $15 \div 2\frac{1}{2} =$ _____

10. $2\frac{1}{2} \div \frac{3}{5} =$ ____

11. $1\frac{3}{4} \div 3\frac{1}{2} =$ _____

12. $1\frac{3}{4} \div 1\frac{1}{2} =$ _____

13. $5\frac{1}{2} \div 3\frac{1}{4} =$ _____

14. $5\frac{5}{8} \div 3\frac{2}{3} =$ _____

15. $3\frac{1}{8} \div 2\frac{2}{9} =$ _____

CARD 1

$2\frac{1}{4}$	$\frac{3}{5}$	$1\frac{47}{88}$
$1\frac{1}{6}$	$7\frac{3}{7}$	$\frac{4}{9}$
$9\frac{1}{3}$	$1\frac{9}{13}$	$\frac{5}{8}$

CARD 2

$7\frac{3}{4}$	$3\frac{2}{3}$	$1\frac{13}{25}$
2	$4\frac{1}{6}$	$\frac{8}{9}$
$\frac{1}{10}$	7	4

CARD 3

6	$3\frac{1}{2}$	$\frac{7}{8}$
$\frac{1}{9}$	$\frac{1}{2}$	17
16	$1\frac{13}{32}$	$\frac{1}{4}$

AND THE WINNING CARD IS ... _____

A Fraction Dictionary

DIRECTIONS: Create a small book to show your understanding of basic fraction concepts and also to share with your friends or other students in your school.

Your book will have 7 pages and a cover. Give your book a title, and then design a clever cover that will grab the reader's attention.

Listed below are ten topics having to do with fractions. Choose any 6 and develop a page in your book for each of those 6 fraction topics. Each page needs to have the topic listed and one or more drawings to illustrate your understanding of that topic. *See "Sample Page".*

Fraction Topics

(1) What is a fraction? Show the numerator and denominator, and how you know the difference.
(2) Equivalent fractions
(3) Reducing fractions to lowest terms
(4) Comparing fractions such as ¼ to ½
(5) Mixed Numbers
(6) Improper Fractions
(7) Adding fractions
(8) Subtracting fractions
(9) Multiplying fractions
(10) Dividing fractions

On the back cover of your book create an *About the Author* page. Tell your readers about yourself. You may want to include your age, your favorite hobbies, and even a picture of yourself.

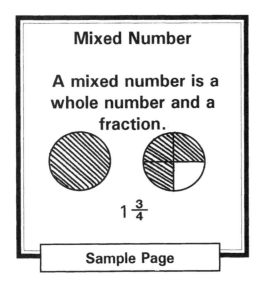

Mixed Number

A mixed number is a whole number and a fraction.

$1\frac{3}{4}$

Sample Page

About the Author

Changing decimal word names to standard decimal numerals

NAME _____

What should you do if your dog starts to chew up your dictionary?

DIRECTIONS: Write each decimal word name as a standard decimal numeral. Each time your answer appears in the decoder, write the letter of the problem above it.

1. Seven and eight tenths = _____ **M**

2. Three and four tenths = _____ **F**

3. Twelve and five hundredths = _____ **U**

4. Eight tenths = _____ **G**

5. One hundred and seven thousandths = _____ **I**

6. Ninety-nine and three hundredths = _____ **S**

7. Forty and forty-five hundredths = _____ **D**

8. Three and one tenth = _____ **R**

9. Four thousand and two tenths = _____ **O**

10. Seven and eight hundredths = _____ **W**

11. Eight thousandths = _____ **E**

12. Four and forty-five hundredths = _____ **H**

13. Ninety and three tenths = _____ **K**

14. One hundred seventeen and five tenths = _____ **A**

15. Thirty-three and four thousandths = _____ **T**

33.004	117.5	90.3	0.008	33.004	4.45	0.008

7.08	4,000.2	3.1	40.45	99.03		

3.1	100.007	0.8	4.45	33.004	4,000.2	12.05	33.004

4,000.2	3.4	4.45	100.007	99.03

7.8	4,000.2	12.05	33.004	4.45

©2000 by Incentive Publications, Inc., Nashville, TN.

52

NAME _____

Determining place value in decimals

What do you call a cow eating grass?

DIRECTIONS: Determine which digit occupies the given place value in each of the decimals below. Find your answer in the decoder. Each time it occurs in the decoder, write the letter of the problem above it.

1. 37.034 (thousandths) = _____ L

2. 63.05 (ones) = _____ E

3. 456.893 (hundredths) = _____ N

4. 0.007 (tenths) = _____ W

5. 878,436.023 (ten thousands) = _____ A

6. 4.091 (thousandths) = _____ R

7. 6,437.832 (tenths) = _____ O

8. 325,678,921.5 (ten millions) = _____ M

___ ___ ___ ___ ___
7   4   7   0   9

___ ___ ___ - ___ ___
2   8   8   3   1

©2000 by Incentive Publications, Inc., Nashville, TN.

CROSS NUMBER PUZZLE

A 3	B 8		C	D	E	
F		G	H	I		J
	K	L	M		N	O
P		Q		R	S	T
U	V	W	X		Y	Z

Try to solve this Cross Number Puzzle!

DIRECTIONS: Complete the puzzle by **rounding** each number given below to the nearest **whole** number. The first one has been done for you.

TRICK! Look at the number immediately to the right of the one's place. That number will be in the tenth's place. If the tenth's place contains a 5 or higher, then you will need to round the number up; however, if the tenth's place contains a number 4 or less you round the number down.

ACROSS

A 37.89 = _____38_____

C 542.39 = _____

F 5.6 = _____

G 907.653 = _____

J 2.99 = _____

K 752.004 = _____

N 60.91 = _____

P 3.06 = _____

Q 5.87 = _____

R 907.08 = _____

U 8,903. 45 = _____

Y 74.6 = _____

DOWN

A 35.9 = _____

B 7.5 = _____

C 502.01 = _____

D 48.435 = _____

E 2.1 = _____

G 9,560.3 = _____

J 3174.6 = _____

K 6.94 = _____

N 607.4 = _____

P 38.009 = _____

R 8.55 = _____

V 9.01 = _____

X 2.6 = _____

Comparing decimals

NAME _____

What happens when you put snakes on a car window?

DIRECTIONS: Choose the greatest number and circle it. Then write the letter underneath your choice in the decoder below.

1. 3.8   3.08
    R   W

2. 44.1   4.41
    P   Z

3. 6.57   7.01
    W   V

4. 0.99   1.00
    B   L

5. 78.09 78.34
    B   T

6. 66.71 7.99
    H   Y

7. 3.01   2.9
    S   Q

8. 5.25   5.2
    D   A

9. 3.89   33.9
    X   N

10. 14.005 14.1
    C   I

11. 3.004 3.1
    G   E

12. 6,351 666.9
    W   F

13. 98.9   99
    H   G

14. 1,001 999
    U   J

15. 0.7   1.1
    M   O

16. 0.004 0.4
    P   Y

99	3.1	78.34

0.4	1.1	1,001		3.01	3.1	1.00	5.25

6,351	14.1	33.9	5.25	3.01	66.71	14.1	3.1		7.01	14.1	44.1	3.1	3.8	3.01

A TRICK for
Adding and Subtracting
DECIMALS

The *TRICK* for adding and subtracting decimals is using a colored pencil or marker to line up the decimal points and using zeros as placeholders to the right of the decimal.

EXAMPLES:

16.8 + 1.95 =	16.8	16.80 (add zero)
	+ 1.95	+ 1.95
(Can't be done!)		18.75 (Now, it can be done!)

9.34 – 0.078 =	9.34	9.340 (add zero)
	- 0.0 78	- 0.078
(Can't be done!)		9.262 (Now, it can be done!)

Let's try a few: *(Answers are in a mixed order at the bottom of the page. All answers are not used.)*

1.   0.01 + 0.010 = _____

2.   2.6 + 30.1 = _____

3.   2.345 + 0.093 = _____

4.   9.34 - 0.078 = _____

5.   84.9 - 9.34 = _____

6.   604.2 - 49.000 = _____

7.   97 - 6.34 = _____

8.   3.45 + 60.2 + 0.98 = _____

Possible Answers:	75.56	90.66	0.02	555.2	9.567
	64.63	32.7	9.262	7.84	2.438

NAME _____

What happened when the canary flew into the fan?

DIRECTIONS: Solve each problem below and find your answer in the decoder. Each time your answer appears in the decoder, write the letter of the problem above it. (REMEMBER! When adding decimals, the decimal points must line up in a vertical (↓) straight row.)

EXAMPLE: $3.4 + 0.78 + 60.03 = 64.21$
You may want to use graph paper to help you line up your decimals.

$$\begin{array}{r} 3.4 \\ 0.78 \\ +60.03 \\ \hline 64.21 \end{array}$$

Decimals are lined up vertically in a straight line.

1. $6.7 + 0.0008 + 9.0 + 0.092 =$ _____ W

2. $1.09 + 8.763 + 0.10 =$ _____ T

3. $0.08 + 2.05 + 0.019 + 6.4 =$ _____ D

4. $0.71 + 3.005 + 34.6 + 0.458 =$ _____ E

5. $0.8 + 0.09 =$ _____ R

6. $4.0 + 0.009 =$ _____ H

7. $0.008 + 1.45 + 0.09 + 4456.0 =$ _____ S

4,457.548	4.009	0.89	38.773	8.549	8.549	38.773	8.549

9.953	15.7928	38.773	38.773	9.953

Adding and subtracting decimals

DECIMAL BINGO

NAME _____

DIRECTIONS: Solve these problems on another sheet of paper. You may want to use graph paper or a colored pencil to help you keep your decimals in a vertical line. After you have solved each problem, find your answer in the DECIMAL BINGO boxes below. Circle each answer you find. When you have circled five answers in a line either horizontally, diagonally or vertically, you have a DECIMAL BINGO.

58

20.06	19.93	8.96	$7.00	9.205
$1.02	$8.75	3.65	5.723	$20.07
7.38	$6.79	FREE SPACE	7.36	25.35
9.7	3.912	22.3	8.7	26.41
$5.11	$8.96	24.75	$6.00	2.993

1. 7.0 + 19.41 = _____

2. 15.75 + 4.18 = _____

3. 15.00 – 7.64 = _____

4. 3.000 – 0.007 = _____

5. 11.175 – 1.970 = _____

6. $10.91 – $9.89 = _____

7. 0.1 + 0.8 + 7.8 = _____

8. 38.5 – 16.2 = _____

9. $8.89 – $2.10 = _____

10. $20.00 – $14.89 = _____

11. 10.00 – 6.35 = _____

12. 94.32 – 68.97 = _____

13. $13.75 + $6.32 = _____

What's the title of this picture?

DIRECTIONS: First, solve each problem below on another sheet of paper. Second, find your answer in the decoder at the bottom of the page. Third, each time your answer appears in the decoder, write the letter of the problem above it.

TIP: You may want to solve these problems using graph paper. Look carefully at the steps that are involved in multiplying decimals:

Step 1: Multiply the numbers as whole numbers.

Step 2: Count the digits to the right of the decimal points in the factors.

Step 3: Count off the same number of digits to place the decimal point in the product.

$$
\begin{array}{r}
1.8 \\
\times\ .7 \\
\hline
126
\end{array}
$$

$$
\begin{array}{r}
1.8 \\
\times\ .7 \\
\hline
\end{array}
$$
Number of digits to the right of the decimal point in the factors is 2.

$$
\begin{array}{r}
1.8 \\
\times\ .7 \\
\hline
1.26
\end{array}
$$
Decimal point is moved 2 places to the left.

1. 7.53 x 0.5 = _____ B

2. 0.498 x 0.14 = _____ D

3. 9.6 x 3.2 = _____ R

4. 50.8 x 0.35 = _____ E

5. 1.56 x 3.4 = _____ A

6. 91.4 x 15.8 = _____ N

7. 18.1 x 0.24 = _____ L

8. 67.4 x 0.47 = _____ S

9. 32 x 8.96 = _____ K

10. 6.52 x 2.4 = _____ U

11. 6.5 x 12 = _____ T

12. 4.32 x 0.02 = _____ O

5.304	78	15.648	30.72	78	4.344	17.78	0.0864	1,444.12	5.304

31.678	286.72	5.304	78	17.78	3.765	0.0864	5.304	30.72	0.06972

Dividing decimals by whole numbers

NAME_____

What did one escalator say to the other escalator?

DIRECTIONS: **First,** solve each problem on another sheet of paper. **Second,** locate your answer in the decoder. **Third,** each time your answer occurs in the decoder, write the letter of the problem above it. Plan to round each quotient to the nearest thousandth. **For example,** if the quotient were 26.2233, your answer would be 26.223. However, if the quotient were 26.2235, your answer would be 26.224.

1. $58.2 \div 6 =$ _____ G

2. $65.23 \div 8 =$ _____ C

3. $0.468 \div 9 =$ _____ W

4. $8.5 \div 5 =$ _____ M

5. $7.8 \div 32 =$ _____ N

6. $5.78 \div 2 =$ _____ H

7. $189.45 \div 74 =$ _____ K

8. $45.8 \div 29 =$ _____ S

9. $20.34 \div 9 =$ _____ T

10. $178.4 \div 16 =$ _____ A

11. $0.0375 \div 5 =$ _____ O

12. $58.422 \div 91 =$ _____ D

13. $157.56 \div 52 =$ _____ E

14. $23.52 \div 98 =$ _____ I

| ___ | ___ | ___ | ___ | ___ | ___ | ___ | ___ | ___ |
| 0.24 | 2.26 | 2.89 | 0.24 | 0.244 | 2.560 | 0.24 | 11.15 | 1.7 |

| ___ | ___ | ___ | ___ | ___ | ___ | ___ | ___ | ___ | ___ |
| 8.154 | 0.008 | 1.7 | 0.24 | 0.244 | 9.7 | 0.642 | 0.008 | 0.052 | 0.244 |

| ___ | ___ | ___ | ___ | ___ | ___ | ___ | ___ | ___ | ___ | ___ | ___ | ___ |
| 0.052 | 0.24 | 2.26 | 2.89 | 1.579 | 0.008 | 1.7 | 3.03 | 2.26 | 2.89 | 0.24 | 0.244 | 9.7 |

NAME _____

What happened to the dog when he ate only garlic and onions?

DIRECTIONS: First, solve each problem on another sheet of paper. **Second,** locate your answer in the decoder. **Third,** each time your answer occurs in the decoder, write the letter of the problem above it. Plan to round each quotient to the nearest hundredth.

1. $0.6 \div 0.325 =$ _____ R

2. $10 \div 0.08 =$ _____ A

3. $0.3225 \div 0.043 =$ _____ N

4. $0.41 \div 1.23 =$ _____ S

5. $843 \div 1.5 =$ _____ T

6. $0.2 \div 0.3 =$ _____ O

7. $3.99 \div 0.019 =$ _____ H

8. $0.05 \div 0.07 =$ _____ E

9. $14.13 \div 0.341 =$ _____ K

10. $0.9 \div 0.84 =$ _____ B

11. $2.45 \div 0.007 =$ _____ I

12. $3 \div 0.41 =$ _____ W

210	350	0.33	1.07	125	125	1.85	41.44	7.32	125	0.33	7.32	0.67	1.85	0.33	0.71

562	210	125	7.5	210	350	0.33	1.07	350	562	0.71

Practicing estimation skills

NAME _____

Let's Play JEOPARDY!

DIRECTIONS: Here's your opportunity to play the popular T.V. show *Jeopardy*. Notice there are 5 categories and below each category is a problem with its estimated answer. If you think the answer is reasonable, circle it with an orange crayon. If you think the answer is too high, circle it with a blue crayon. If you think the estimate is too low, circle it with a green crayon. DO NOT SOLVE ANY PROBLEMS ON PAPER; JUST ESTIMATE IN YOUR HEAD!

Points	ADDITION	SUBTRACTION	MULTIPLICATION	DIVISION	DECIMALS
10	413 + 345 = 800	Ben had $50.00. He spent $25.99 on a soccer ball, and $3.49 on baseball cards. How much did he have left? About $21.00 left	16 x 34 = 400	69 ÷ 9 = 7	3.45 12.60 + 9.44 28.00
20	67 +81 150	5,234 - 2,876 = 3,000	Colored markers are $0.29 each. You bought 8. How much did you spend? About $3.40	6 students on a team. 55 students in all. How many teams in all About 8 teams in all	$382.65 - $78.89 = $200
30	234 + (453 + 67) = 900	34,876 - 23,567 1,000	6 x (32 x 8) = 1,800	334 ÷ 64 = 50	4.56 x 2.67 15.00
40	$1.09 4.65 + 17.85 $25.00	$345.69 - $98.65 = $75.00	37 x 47 1,600	90 67)679	23.67 ÷ 3.57 = 6.00
50	32,456 65,923 + 5,678 90,000	If you had $33.98 and you received $10 from your grandparents, and then spent $25.98 on a new sweater, how much would you have left? About $18 left	How many eggs are in 12 dozen? 200 eggs	$24.95 for 4 CDs. How much for one? About $6.00 each	2.34 + 67.43 + 8.2 = 88

Use your calculator and check your answer. For every correct answer give yourself the number of points that it is worth. What was your total? _____ 700 points to 750 points is *Outstanding!* 600 to 699 points is *Excellent!* 500 to 599 is *Very Good*. Keep practicing those estimation skills because you'll find you will use them everyday in your daily life.

ROAD KILL CAFÉ MENU

FOOD ITEM	*PRICE (before tax)*

Appetizers

Fried Mosquito Wings	$0.25 (a pair)

Boiled Squirrel Stew

Large Bowl	$2.10
Small Bowl	$1.49

Wild Pig Snouts (marinated and then grilled)

6 snouts	$1.80
12 snouts	$3.50

Turtle Soup	$1.50

Salads

Roadside Salad (A mixture of delicious weeds)	$1.80

Main Dishes

Possum Steak	$3.35
Barbecued Raccoon Ribs	$2.80
Snake Kabobs	$3.40
Spider Web Soufflé	$1.80
Mystery Burger with all the trimmings	$1.65
Cajun Rabbit Steak	$2.90

Drinks

Bugjuice Cola	$0.75
Sweet Puddle Diet Drink	$0.35

Desserts

Skunk-Flavored Popsicle	$0.75

Chocolate Covered Frog Legs

10 legs	$2.25
20 legs	$4.00

Sugar Coated Dragonfly Eyeball Surprise	$1.25

We hope you have enjoyed your meal. Please tell your friends about us and come back for more delicious "road kill" special delights.

DIRECTIONS: Use your calculator to help you solve the following problems using the Road Kill Café Menu.

1. You have $5.00 to spend for dinner. Spend as much as you can without going over the $5.00 limit. List the items, cost, total amount and any change you will receive.

ITEM	COST
_____	_____
_____	_____
_____	_____
_____	_____
_____	_____

Total cost: _____

Change received: _____

2. Derrick bought 6 of the same item and the total price was $1.50. What did he buy? _____

3. Nikki had five items for dinner: meat, drink, salad, soup, and dessert. Her total price was $7.20. What did she order ?_____

_____

4. Would it be more economical to buy four orders of 10 Chocolate Covered Frog Legs, or two orders of 20 Chocolate Covered Frog legs? _____
Explain._____

5. If you had $7.00 to spend on dinner, would you have enough money to order an appetizer of 6 Pig Snouts, Barbecued Raccoon Ribs, Bugjuice Cola, Roadside Salad, and a Skunk Flavored Popsicle? _____ Explain. _____

_____

6. Your family has decided to have a Sampler Party so they can taste each delicious item. Calculate the total cost. Choose the smallest servings for those items that have choices on sizes. Add in a 0.07% sales tax. Will $30.00 be sufficient? Yes _____ No _____

Cost :_____

Sales tax: _____

Total Cost: _____

NAME_____

What did one calendar say to the other calendar?

DIRECTIONS: Solve each proportion and find your answer in the decoder at the bottom of the page. Each time your answer appears in the decoder, write the letter of the problem above it.

1.   1 : 2 = T : 6
     T = _____

2.   2 : 5 = 10 : H
     H = _____

3.   6 : 5 = S : 15
     S = _____

4.   10 : 7 = 50 : V
     V = _____

5.   3 : 7 = 6 : R
     R = _____

6.   3 : 1 = U : 10
     U = _____

7.   4 : 3 = Y : 30
     Y = _____

8.   4 : 25 = 8 : I
     I = _____

9.   3 : 8 = 30 : N
     N = _____

10. 1 : 3 = 4 : E
     E = _____

11. 5 : 4 = 20 : O
     O = _____

12. 5 : 11 = 10 : M
     M = _____

13. 7 : 4 = A : 16
     A = _____

14. 5 : 7 = D : 14
     D = _____

| 50 | 25 | 28 | 35 | 12 | | 22 | 16 | 14 | 12 |

| 10 | 28 | 3 | 12 | 18 | | 3 | 25 | 28 | 80 |

| 40 | 16 | 30 | | 10 | 16 |

Which president do monkeys like best?

DIRECTIONS: First, write a ratio in lowest terms for each problem below. **Second,** find the ratio given in fractional form at the bottom of the page. **Third,** each time the ratio appears in the decoder, write the letter above it. See the example given below.

> **Number of letters in *Olympics* to the number of letters in *motorcycle* :**
>
> ***Olympics*** has 8 letters; ***motorcycle*** has 10 letters.
>
> The ratio is $\frac{8}{10}$ which can be reduced to $\frac{4}{5}$.

1. **Number of letters in *Dalmatian* to the number of letters in *dog*** = _____ (I)

2. **Number of letters in *space* to the number of letters in *hamburgers*** = _____ (N)

3. **Number of letters in *baseball* to the number of letters in *encyclopedia*** = _____ (E)

4. **Number of letters in *candy* to the number of letters in *soccer*** = _____ (C)

5. **Number of letters in *basketball* to the number of letters in *elephant*** = _____ (P)

6. **Number of letters in *love* to the number of letters in *friendship*** = _____ (L)

7. **Number of letters in *popcorn* to the number of letters in *diamond*** = _____ (A)

8. **Number of letters in *dollar* to the number of letters in *dime*** = _____ (O)

$$\frac{\rule{1cm}{0.4pt}}{\frac{1}{1}} \quad \frac{\rule{1cm}{0.4pt}}{\frac{5}{4}} \quad \frac{\rule{1cm}{0.4pt}}{\frac{2}{3}}$$

$$\frac{\rule{1cm}{0.4pt}}{\frac{2}{5}} \quad \frac{\rule{1cm}{0.4pt}}{\frac{3}{1}} \quad \frac{\rule{1cm}{0.4pt}}{\frac{1}{2}} \quad \frac{\rule{1cm}{0.4pt}}{\frac{5}{6}} \quad \frac{\rule{1cm}{0.4pt}}{\frac{3}{2}} \quad \frac{\rule{1cm}{0.4pt}}{\frac{2}{5}} \quad \frac{\rule{1cm}{0.4pt}}{\frac{1}{2}}$$

NAME _____

Using graphs to determine percent

Where do geologists go for entertainment?

DIRECTIONS: Find the percent of each graph that is shaded. Each time your answer occurs in the decoder, write the letter of the problem above it.

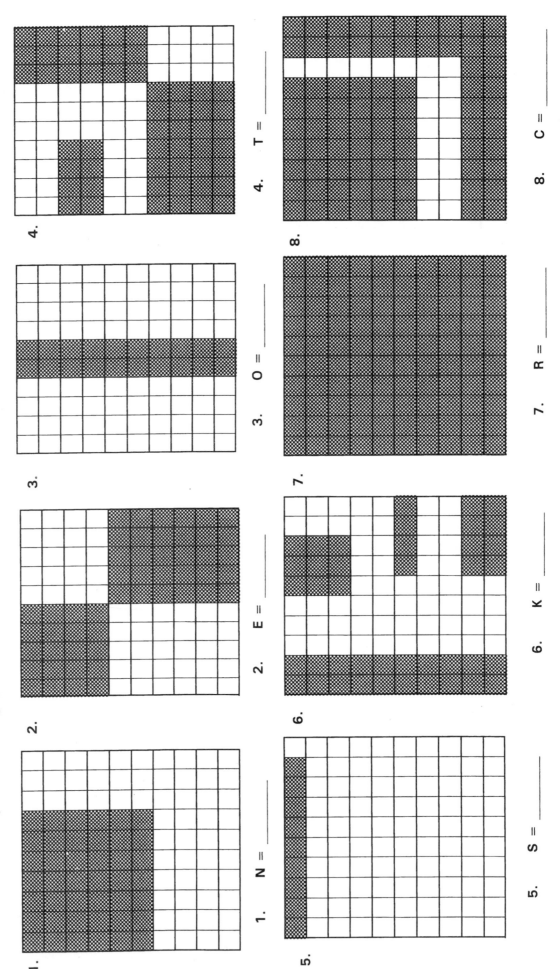

1. _____

2. _____

3. _____

4. T = _____

5. _____

6. _____

7. _____

8. _____

54%	20%	100%	78%	41%		78%	20%	42%	78%	50%	100%	54%	9%
	S =		N =			K =		R =			C =		

1. 2. 3. 4. 5. 6. 7. 8.

N = _____   E = _____   O = _____   K = _____   S = _____   R = _____   C = _____

Who couldn't get their airplane to fly?

DIRECTIONS: First, change any percent below into a fraction in lowest terms. Second, each time this fraction appears in the decoder, write the letter of that problem above it.

Example: $30\% = \frac{30}{100} = \frac{3}{10}$

1. 10% = _____ (R)   6. 2% = _____ (N)

2. 40% = _____ (G)   7. 13% = _____ (O)

3. 35% = _____ (E)   8. 25% = _____ (B)

4. 80% = _____ (T)   9. 60% = _____ (H)

5. 12% = _____ (S)   10. 1% = _____ (W)

$\frac{4}{5}$ $\frac{3}{5}$ $\frac{7}{20}$ $\frac{1}{100}$ $\frac{1}{10}$ $\frac{13}{100}$ $\frac{1}{50}$ $\frac{2}{5}$

$\frac{1}{4}$ $\frac{1}{10}$ $\frac{13}{100}$ $\frac{4}{5}$ $\frac{3}{5}$ $\frac{7}{20}$ $\frac{1}{10}$ $\frac{3}{25}$

NAME _____

How does St. Peter greet you as you approach the gates?

DIRECTIONS: Use the *given price* and the *percent discount* to find the *SALE* price in each problem. Then find your answer in the decoder, and write the letter of the problem above it. An example has been done for you.

$6.00; 25% discount = _____ **(Sale Price)**

$6.00
x .25
3000
12000
$1.5000

$1.50 is discounted from the regular price
$6.00 - $1.50 = $4.50. The sale price is $4.50.

(4 decimal places in your two factors; so, counting 4 places from the right would mean the decimal needed to put between the 1 and 5).

---

1. $5.00; 20% discount = _____ (R)

2. $16.00; 5% discount = _____ (W)

3. $11.00; 25% discount = _____ (O)

4. $17.00; 50% discount = _____ (A)

5. $5.50; 10% discount = _____ (T)

6. $75.00; 75% discount = _____ (E)

7. $100.00; 60% discount = _____ (L)

8. $8.00; 70% discount = _____ (H)

_____ _____ _____ _____ , _____ _____ _____ _____
$15.20 $18.75 $40 $40 $2.40 $8.50 $40 $8.25

_____ _____ _____ _____ _____
$4.95 $2.40 $18.75 $4 $18.75

Movin' On!

Can you help the timekeeper at Running With the Wind Middle School? He always does a fantastic job, but right now he has a problem. He forgot to write down the name of each runner's team.

DIRECTIONS: Using the lap times and the clues given, can you help him complete the table at the bottom of the page? Don't forget: the *fastest* time for a lap is the *lowest* number. *The first one has been done for you.*

TIME (in seconds)

Lap 1	Lap 2	Lap 3	Lap 4
63.4	57.36	61.39	59.76
61.09	65.6	69.7	62.3
58.07	64.4	59.2	66.35
62.4	60.08	60.23	64.75
59.16	62.4	60.58	55.88 *Team 4*

1. Team 4 ran the fastest 4th lap.
2. Team 5 ran the fastest 2nd lap.
3. Team 3 ran the slowest 2nd lap.
4. Team 4 ran the fastest 1st lap and 3rd lap.
5. Team 1 ran 1 second faster than Team 2 in Lap 1.
6. Team 5 ran the 2nd fastest Lap 1 and Lap 4.
7. Team 1 had the 2nd fastest Lap 2.
8. Team 2 had the slowest Lap 3 and Lap 4.

9. In Lap 3, Team 3 ran faster than Team 1 by .35 seconds.
10. In Lap 4, Team 1 came in 3rd.
11. Team 3's time in Lap 1 was faster than Team 5's time in Lap 3.
12. Team 2's time in Lap 2 was 2.0 seconds faster than Team 4.
13. In Lap 4 Team 3 came in 4th.

TEAM	Lap 1	Lap 2	Lap 3	Lap 4	Total
1					
2					
3					
4				55.88	
5					

Use your calculator and help the scorekeeper find the winning team!
The winner is _____

NAME_____

MEASUREMENT MAN

Materials: construction paper, scissors, ruler, markers, glue

Directions: Using the drawing of Measurement Man, ask students to use different colored construction paper for each measurement, and then cut and glue the correlating pieces of construction paper onto the drawing, or make a larger scale version of the Measurement Man.

An easy way to remember liquid measurement from the smallest to the largest is to look at the size of the words! The smallest measurement, the cup, has 3 letters, which makes it smaller than a pint (4 letters).

c-u-p = 3 letters   q-u-a-r-t = 5 letters
p-i-n-t = 4 letters   g-a-l-l-o-n = 6 letters

Below are given the corresponding standard measurement pieces that are found on the Measurement Man.

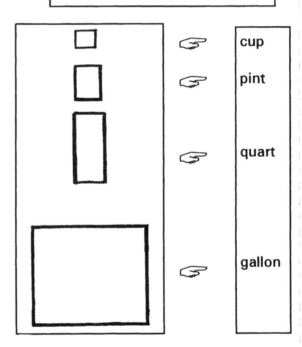

cup

pint

quart

gallon

Use your Measurement Man to solve these problems:

1. 4 pints = _____ quarts

2. 2 gallons = _____ pints

3. 4 gallons = _____ quarts

4. 8 cups = _____ quarts

5. 4 quarts = _____ gallon

6. 8 pints = _____ quarts

7. 1 gallon = _____ pints

8. 4 pints = _____ cups

STUDENT RECORDING SHEET

DIRECTIONS: With a partner, complete your body measurements using the metric system. You will need a metric tape, a friend, and a pencil. Have fun!

HEIGHT

Estimate _____

Actual _____

ARM SPAN

Estimate _____

Actual _____

LENGTH OF THUMB

Estimate _____

Actual _____

AROUND WAIST

Estimate _____

Actual _____

WIDTH OF SMILE

Estimate _____

Actual _____

LENGTH OF FOOT

Estimate _____

Actual _____

METRIC MAN

LENGTH OF BIG TOE

Estimate _____

Actual _____

LENGTH OF ARM

Estimate _____

Actual _____

AROUND WRIST

Estimate _____

Actual _____

LENGTH OF LEG

Estimate _____

Actual _____

AROUND HEAD

Estimate _____

Actual _____

AROUND NECK

Estimate _____

Actual _____

Should we weigh this ball in grams, kilograms, or milligrams?

NAME _____

Decisions, Decisions, Decisions

DIRECTIONS: For each item listed, choose the most appropriate measurement from the list in each of the three boxes. Write your answer in the space provided.

> **Measurement of Length:**
> meter (m), millimeter (mm), centimeter (cm), kilometer (km)

1. the length of a math book _____
2. the distance from San Francisco, CA to Portland, OR _____
3. the width of a mosquito's leg _____
4. the distance from Earth to Pluto _____
5. the height of a football goal post _____
6. the width of your toenail _____
7. the length of your bicycle _____
8. the width of your ear lobe _____
9. the length of a swimming pool _____
10. the distance run by a marathoner _____

> **Liquid Measurement**
> Liter (L), milliliter (mL)

> **Measurement of Mass:**
> gram (g), milligram (mg), kilogram (kg)

11. a drop of water _____
12. a carton of lemonade _____
13. a swimming pool _____
14. a medicine dropper _____
15. a melted ice cube _____
16. a bathtub of hot water _____
17. a jug of milk _____
18. a spoonful of medicine _____

19. a peacock feather _____
20. a watermelon _____
21. an elephant _____
22. a coffee cup _____
23. a shoelace _____
24. a computer _____
25. YOU! _____
26. a fly's wing _____

NAME _____

What is the title of this picture?

DIRECTIONS: Using the information given in the chart below, solve the problems involving standard measurement. Each time your answer appears in the decoder, write the letter of the problem above it.

TRICK: If the problem requires you to go from "big" to "small", you'll need to multiply; however, if the problem requires you to go from "small" to "big", then you'll divide.

Remember this saying:
Big to small, multiply all!
Small to big, divide the pig!

Length	Liquid Measurement	Weight	Time
12 inches = 1 foot 3 feet = 1 yard or 36 inches = 1 yard 5,280 feet = 1 mile or 1,760 yards = 1 mile	2 cups = 1 pint 2 pints = 1 quart 4 quarts = 1 gallon	16 ounces = 1 pound (lb) 2000 pounds = 1 ton	60 seconds = 1 minute 60 minutes = 1 hour 24 hours = 1 day 7 days = 1 week

1. 7 ft. 3 inches = _____ inches (R)

2. 4,032 inches = _____ yards (N)

3. 3½ days = _____ hours (T)

4. 1 pound 8 ounces = _____ ounces (I)

5. 13 pints = _____ cups (E)

6. 156 inches = _____ feet (A)

7. 5 gallons = _____ pints (H)

8. 5,280 yards = _____ miles (U)

9. 154 days = _____ weeks (K)

10. 3¼ hours = _____ minutes (C)

11. 6½ tons = _____ lb. (O)

| 13 | 195 | 40 | 24 | 195 | 22 | 26 | 112 | | 13,000 | 112 |

| 13,000 | 112 | 26 | | 195 | 87 | 3 | 84 | 195 | 40 |

NAME _____

DESIGNING WITH AREA

Using graph paper to show area

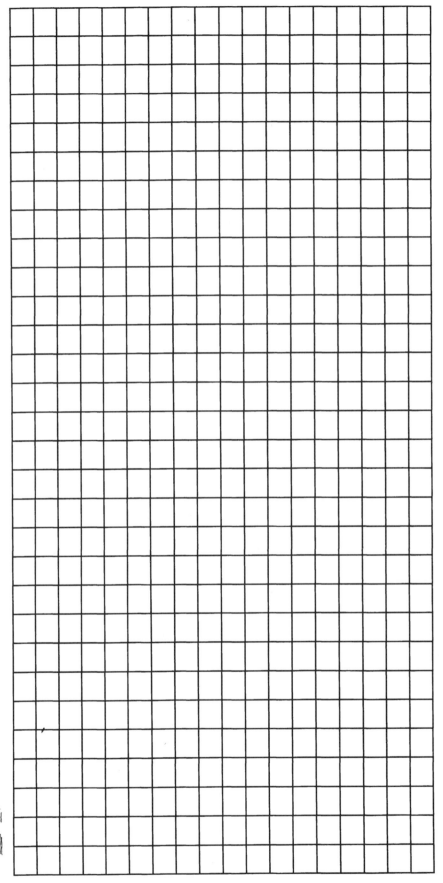

Do you think
our Earth has
a very large
area?

DIRECTIONS: Use your imagination and design shapes on the graph paper that will show you understand the concept of area.

1. Create 2 different shapes that have an area of **16 square units.**

2. Create 2 different shapes that have an area of **33 square units.**

3. Create 1 shape that has an area of **40 or more square units.**

What is the area of your largest shape ? _____

Where's the best place to see a man-eating fish?

DIRECTIONS: Use your protractor to measure each angle. Each time the measurement of your angle appears in the decoder, write the letter of the problem above it. *Remember: Ask yourself is the angle less than or greater than 90° before you measure it. This information will help you decide what numbers on the protractor to use.*

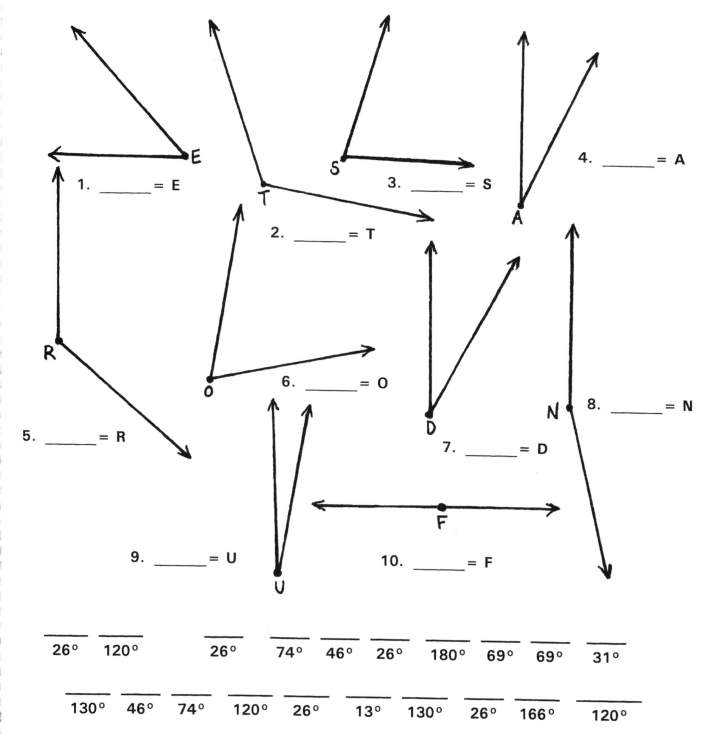

1. _____ = E

2. _____ = T

3. _____ = S

4. _____ = A

5. _____ = R

6. _____ = O

7. _____ = D

8. _____ = N

9. _____ = U

10. _____ = F

___ ___   ___ ___ ___ ___ ___ ___ ___ ___
26° 120°   26° 74° 46° 26° 180° 69° 69° 31°

___ ___ ___ ___ ___   ___ ___ ___ ___   ___
130° 46° 74° 120° 26°   13° 130° 26° 166°   120°

NAME _____

Finding evidences of geometric shapes

A Geometry Scavenger Hunt

DIRECTIONS: On your scavenger hunt look for examples of the following geometric figures in your environment and then illustrate in the boxes below one example for each geometric figure listed. A drawing is given for each figure to help you.

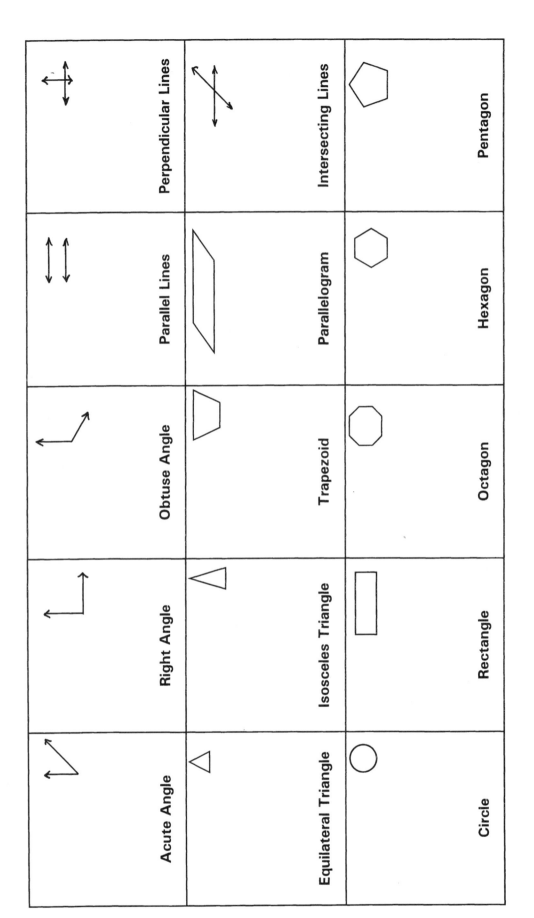

Acute Angle	Right Angle	Obtuse Angle	Parallel Lines	Perpendicular Lines
Equilateral Triangle	Isosceles Triangle	Trapezoid	Parallelogram	Intersecting Lines
Circle	Rectangle	Octagon	Hexagon	Pentagon

Finding area and volume

NAME _____

What did the doctor prescribe for the bald rabbit?

DIRECTIONS: **First,** find the area or volume of the geometric figures shown below. **Second,** find the answer in the decoder, and each time the answer occurs write the letter of the problem above it.

TIP: **Area** is found by multiplying the length times the width of a given figure.
Answer is expressed in **square** units.

Volume is found by multiplying the length times the width times the height of a given figure.
Answer is expressed in **cubic** units.

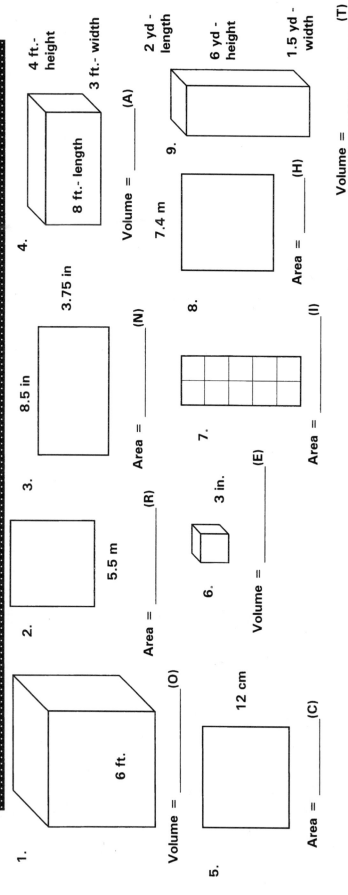

4. 4 ft.- height, 8 ft.- length, 3 ft.- width

Volume = _____ (A)

9. 2 yd - length, 6 yd - height, 1.5 yd - width

Volume = _____ (T)

3. 8.5 in, 3.75 in

Area = _____ (N)

8. 7.4 m

Area = _____ (H)

2. 5.5 m

Area = _____ (R)

7.

Area = _____ (I)

1. 6 ft.

Volume = _____ (O)

5. 12 cm

Area = _____ (C)

6. 3 in.

Volume = _____ (E)

54.76 square meters	96 cubic feet	30.25 square meters	27 cubic inches	18 cubic yards	216 cubic feet	31.875 square inches	10 square units	144 square centimeters

Finding perimeter

What did the digital watch say to its mother?

NAME _____

DIRECTIONS: **First,** find the perimeter of each figure. **Second,** locate your answer in the decoder. **Third,** each time your answer appears in the decoder write the letter of the problem above it.

TIP: Perimeter is found by adding the distance around all of the figure's sides.

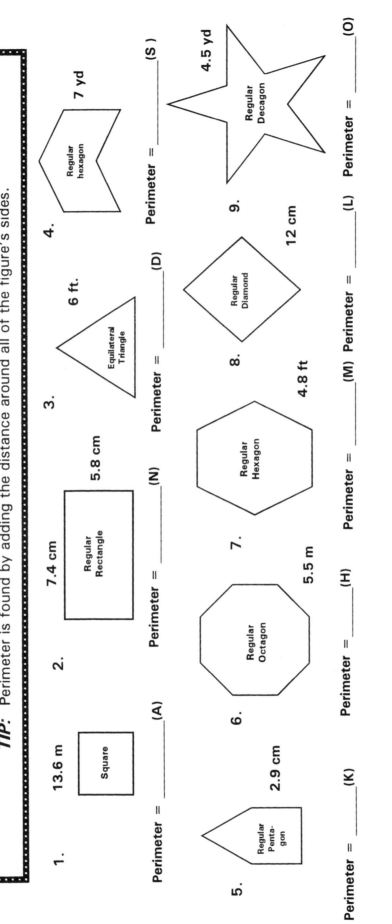

1. 13.6 m

    Square

    Perimeter = _____ (A)

2. 7.4 cm

    5.8 cm

    Regular Rectangle

    Perimeter = _____ (N)

3. 6 ft.

    Equilateral Triangle

    Perimeter = _____ (D)

4. 7 yd

    Regular hexagon

    Perimeter = _____ (S)

5. 2.9 cm

    Regular Penta-gon

    Perimeter = _____ (K)

6. Regular Octagon

    5.5 m

    Perimeter = _____ (H)

7. Regular Hexagon

    4.8 ft

    Perimeter = _____ (M)

8. Regular Diamond

    12 cm

    Perimeter = _____ (L)

9. 4.5 yd

    Regular Decagon

    Perimeter = _____ (O)

_____ _____ _____ _____ _____ ' _____
48 cm 45 yd 45 yd 14.5 cm 45 yd 28.8 ft 54.4 m

_____ _____ _____ _____ _____
26.4 cm 45 yd 44 m 54.4 m 26.4 cm 18 ft 42 yd

APPENDIX:

CHARTS, GRIDS, AND WHOLE NUMBER SPEED SKILL TESTS

MULTIPLICATION FACTS

X	0	1	2	3	4	5	6	7	8	9	10	11	12
0	0	0	0	0	0	0	0	0	0	0	0	0	0
1	0	1	2	3	4	5	6	7	8	9	10	11	12
2	0	2	4	6	8	10	12	14	16	18	20	22	24
3	0	3	6	9	12	15	18	21	24	27	30	33	36
4	0	4	8	12	16	20	24	28	32	36	40	44	48
5	0	5	10	15	20	25	30	35	40	45	50	55	60
6	0	6	12	18	24	30	36	42	48	54	60	66	72
7	0	7	14	21	28	35	42	49	56	63	70	77	84
8	0	8	16	24	32	40	48	56	64	72	80	88	96
9	0	9	18	27	36	45	54	63	72	81	90	99	108
10	0	10	20	30	40	50	60	70	80	90	100	110	120
11	0	11	22	33	44	55	66	77	88	99	110	121	132
12	0	12	24	36	48	60	72	84	96	108	120	132	144

A Table of Factors

1 = 1 x 1	23 = 23 x 1	41 = 1 x 41	57 = 57 x 1	72 = 1 x 72	86 = 1 x 86
2 = 2 x 1			= 3 x 19	= 2 x 36	= 2 x 43
3 = 3 x 1	24 = 1 x 24	42 = 1 x 42		= 3 x 24	
	= 2 x 12	= 2 x 21	58 = 1 x 58	= 4 x 18	87 = 1 x 87
4 = 1 x 4	= 3 x 8	= 3 x 14	= 2 x 29	= 6 x 12	= 3 x 29
= 2 x 2	= 4 x 6	= 6 x 7		= 8 x 9	
			59 = 1 x 59		88 = 1 x 88
5 = 1 x 5	25 = 1 x 25	43 = 1 x 43		73 = 1 x 73	= 2 x 44
	= 5 x 5		60 = 1 x 60		= 4 x 22
6 = 1 x 6		44 = 1 x 44	= 2 x 30	74 = 1 x 74	= 8 x 11
= 2 x 3	26 = 1 x 26	= 2 x 22	= 3 x 20	= 2 x 37	
	= 2 x 13	= 4 x 11	= 4 x 15		89 = 1 x 89
7 = 7 x 1			= 5 x 12	75 = 1 x 75	
	27 = 1 x 27	45 = 1 x 45	= 6 x 10	= 3 x 25	90 = 1 x 90
8 = 1 x 8	= 3 x 9	= 5 x 9		= 5 x 15	= 2 x 45
= 2 x 4			61 = 1 x 61		= 3 x 30
	28 = 1 x 28	46 = 1 x 46		76 = 1 x 76	= 5 x 18
9 = 1 x 9	= 2 x 14	= 2 x 23	62 = 1 x 62	= 2 x 38	= 6 x 15
= 3 x 3	= 4 x 7		= 2 x 31	= 4 x 19	= 9 x 10
		47 = 1 x 47			
10 = 1 x 10	29 = 1 x 29		63 = 1 x 63	77 = 1 x 77	91 = 1 x 91
= 5 x 2		48 = 1 x 48	= 7 x 9	= 7 x 11	= 7 x 13
	30 = 1 x 30	= 2 x 24			
11 = 1 x 11	= 2 x 15	= 3 x 16	64 = 1 x 64	78 = 1 x 78	92 = 1 x 92
	= 3 x 10	= 4 x 12	= 2 x 32	= 2 x 39	= 2 x 46
12 = 1 x 12	= 5 x 6	= 6 x 8	= 4 x 16	= 3 x 26	= 4 x 23
= 2 x 6			= 8 x 8	= 6 x 13	
= 3 x 4	31 = 1 x 31	49 = 1 x 49			93 = 1 x 93
		= 7 x 7	65 = 1 x 65	79 = 1 x 79	= 3 x 31
13 = 1 x 13	32 = 1 x 32		= 5 x 13		
	= 2 x 16	50 = 1 x 50		80 = 1 x 80	94 = 1 x 94
14 = 1 x 14	= 4 x 8	= 2 x 25	66 = 1 x 66	= 2 x 40	= 2 x 47
= 2 x 7		= 5 x 10	= 2 x 33	= 4 x 20	
	33 = 1 x 33		= 6 x 11	= 5 x 16	95 = 1 x 95
15 = 1 x 15	= 3 x 11	51 = 1 x 51	= 3 x 22	= 8 x 10	= 5 x 19
= 3 x 5		= 3 x 17			
	34 = 1 x 34		67 = 1 x 67	81 = 1 x 81	96 = 1 x 96
16 = 1 x 16	= 2 x 17	52 = 1 x 52		= 9 x 9	= 2 x 48
= 2 x 8		= 2 x 26	68 = 1 x 68	= 3 x 27	= 3 x 32
= 4 x 4	35 = 1 x 35	= 4 x 13	= 2 x 34		= 4 x 24
	= 5 x 7		= 4 x 17	82 = 1 x 82	= 6 x 16
17 = 1 x 17		53 = 1 x 53		= 2 x 41	= 8 x 12
	36 = 1 x 36		69 = 1 x 69		
18 = 1 x 18	= 2 x 18	54 = 1 x 54	= 3 x 23	83 = 1 x 83	97 = 1 x 97
= 2 x 9	= 3 x 12	= 2 x 27			
= 3 x 6	= 4 x 9	= 3 x 18	70 = 1 x 70	84 = 1 x 84	98 = 1 x 98
	= 6 x 6	= 6 x 9	= 2 x 35	= 2 x 42	= 2 x 49
19 = 1 x 19			= 5 x 14	= 3 x 28	= 7 x 14
	37 = 1 x 37	55 = 1 x 55	= 7 x 10	= 4 x 21	
20 = 1 x 20		= 5 x 11		= 7 x 12	99 = 1 x 99
= 2 x 10	38 = 1 x 38		71 = 1 x 71	= 6 x 14	= 3 x 33
= 4 x 5	= 2 x 19	56 = 1 x 56			= 9 x 11
		= 2 x 28		85 = 1 x 85	
21 = 1 x 21	39 = 1 x 39	= 4 x 14		= 5 x 17	100 = 1 x 100
= 3 x 7		= 7 x 8			= 2 x 50
	40 = 1 x 40				= 4 x 25
22 = 1 x 22	= 2 x 20				= 5 x 20
= 2 x 11	= 4 x 10				= 10 x 10
	= 5 x 8				

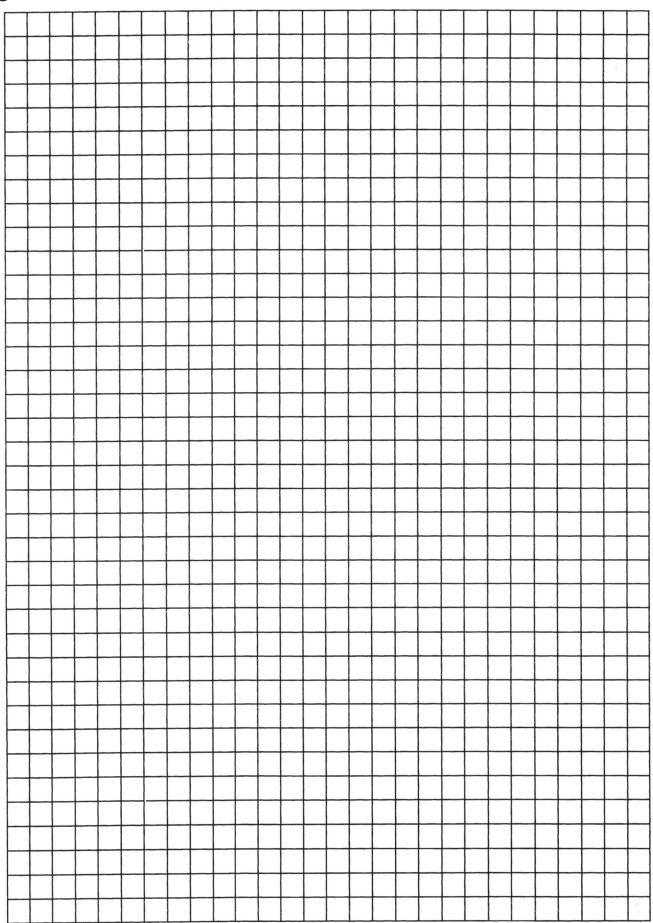

NAME _____ DATE _____

SCORE _____

100 ADDITION FACTS SPEED TEST

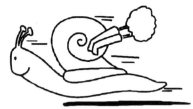

DIRECTIONS: Building your speed in knowing your addition facts can help you improve your computation skills. Try to complete as many of these as you can in 5-10 minutes and then practice those that are difficult for you.

9 + 9 = _____	8 + 1 = _____	1 + 2 = _____	9 + 7 = _____
0 + 0 = _____	2 + 9 = _____	3 + 3 = _____	2 + 0 = _____
8 + 9 = _____	7 + 3 = _____	4 + 0 = _____	1 + 4 = _____
4 + 9 = _____	8 + 5 = _____	6 + 6 = _____	6 + 9 = _____
2 + 3 = _____	9 + 6 = _____	5 + 8 = _____	8 + 6 = _____
7 + 4 = _____	5 + 5 = _____	8 + 0 = _____	6 + 1 = _____
4 + 8 = _____	6 + 0 = _____	7 + 2 = _____	9 + 5 = _____
1 + 9 = _____	4 + 6 = _____	1 + 4 = _____	3 + 1 = _____
4 + 2 = _____	8 + 8 = _____	9 + 8 = _____	2 + 6 = _____
6 + 3 = _____	7 + 6 = _____	3 + 6 = _____	5 + 0 = _____
7 + 7 = _____	6 + 4 = _____	4 + 7 = _____	1 + 5 = _____
3 + 2 = _____	5 + 2 = _____	1 + 0 = _____	2 + 6 = _____
9 + 3 = _____	1 + 1 = _____	7 + 5 = _____	5 + 0 = _____
6 + 8 = _____	3 + 9 = _____	9 + 2 = _____	2 + 8 = _____
3 + 0 = _____	7 + 1 = _____	5 + 9 = _____	6 + 2 = _____
2 + 5 = _____	8 + 7 = _____	6 + 0 = _____	5 + 7 = _____
8 + 3 = _____	1 + 6 = _____	5 + 4 = _____	9 + 1 = _____
7 + 9 = _____	8 + 2 = _____	1 + 7 = _____	4 + 8 = _____
5 + 6 = _____	2 + 1 = _____	4 + 0 = _____	2 + 2 = _____
1 + 8 = _____	4 + 3 = _____	4 + 5 = _____	4 + 4 = _____
3 + 4 = _____	3 + 5 = _____	2 + 4 = _____	3 + 9 = _____
7 + 0 = _____	8 + 4 = _____	1 + 3 = _____	9 + 0 = _____
2 + 7 = _____	6 + 5 = _____	6 + 7 = _____	1 + 5 = _____
3 + 8 = _____	5 + 3 = _____	9 + 4 = _____	2 + 0 = _____
4 + 1 = _____	8 + 0 = _____	5 + 1 = _____	9 + 2 = _____

NAME _____ DATE _____

SCORE _____

100 SUBTRACTION FACTS SPEED TEST

DIRECTIONS: Building your speed in knowing your subtraction facts can help you improve your computation skills. Try to complete as many of these as you can in 5-10 minutes and then practice those that are difficult for you.

9 – 2 = _____	9 – 6 = _____	11 – 8 = _____	17 – 8 = _____
12 – 8 = _____	9 – 7 = _____	12 – 9 = _____	10 – 7 = _____
6 – 6 = _____	11 – 2 = _____	9 – 3 = _____	2 – 1 = _____
8 – 5 = _____	16 – 8 = _____	6 – 4 = _____	5 – 0 = _____
12 – 3 = _____	16 – 7 = _____	2 – 0 = _____	9 – 5 = _____
10 – 9 = _____	9 – 0 = _____	7 – 5 = _____	8 – 4 = _____
13 – 7 = _____	12 – 5 = _____	11 – 6 = _____	16 – 9 = _____
14 – 6 = _____	8 – 6 = _____	15 – 9 = _____	15 – 8 = _____
5 – 2 = _____	8 – 8 = _____	14 – 8 = _____	9 – 1 = _____
5 – 1 = _____	13 – 9 = _____	10 – 1 = _____	8 – 2 = _____
10 – 8 = _____	3 – 1 = _____	13 – 8 = _____	6 – 3 = _____
12 – 7 = _____	8 – 3 = _____	18 – 9 = _____	1 – 1 = _____
13 – 5 = _____	13 – 4 = _____	6 – 5 = _____	8 – 7 = _____
8 – 0 = _____	14 – 5 = _____	1 – 0 = _____	7 – 7 = _____
13 – 6 = _____	12 – 6 = _____	5 – 4 = _____	7 – 1 = _____
15 – 7 = _____	14 – 7 = _____	7 – 2 = _____	6 – 2 = _____
6 – 0 = _____	3 – 0 = _____	17 – 9 = _____	0 – 0 = _____
7 – 4 = _____	11 – 5 = _____	11 – 7 = _____	4 – 2 = _____
5 – 3 = _____	8 – 1 = _____	4 – 3 = _____	10 – 6 = _____
9 – 8 = _____	10 – 3 = _____	9 – 4 = _____	4 – 4 = _____
14 – 9 = _____	5 – 5 = _____	4 – 0 = _____	3 – 2 = _____
4 – 1 = _____	10 – 5 = _____	7 – 3 = _____	15 – 6 = _____
15 – 6 = _____	11 – 9 = _____	3 – 3 = _____	7 – 0 = _____
2 – 2 = _____	7 – 6 = _____	10 – 2 = _____	6 – 1 = _____
10 – 4 = _____	11 – 4 = _____	9 – 9 = _____	12 – 4 = _____

NAME _____ DATE _____

SCORE _____

100 MULTIPLICATION FACTS SPEED TEST

DIRECTIONS: Building your speed in knowing your multiplication facts can help you improve your computation skills. Try to complete as many of these as you can in 5-10 minutes and then practice those that are difficult for you.

5 x 0 = _____	3 x 9 = _____	9 x 9 = _____	8 x 7 = _____
6 x 10 = _____	8 x 1 = _____	1 x 11 = _____	2 x 9 = _____
4 x 12 = _____	3 x 8 = _____	5 x 10 = _____	8 x 5 = _____
8 x 11 = _____	8 x 9 = _____	0 x 8 = _____	6 x 1 = _____
1 x 2 = _____	7 x 10 = _____	5 x 11 = _____	0 x 12 = _____
9 x 4 = _____	2 x 2 = _____	7 x 2 = _____	7 x 6 = _____
2 x 11 = _____	7 x 12 = _____	6 x 4 = _____	4 x 3 = _____
4 x 6 = _____	4 x 7 = _____	2 x 7 = _____	4 x 4 = _____
6 x 8 = _____	3 x 4 = _____	5 x 3 = _____	7 x 5 = _____
1 x 8 = _____	5 x 4 = _____	9 x 8 = _____	6 x 11 = _____
9 x 6 = _____	6 x 5 = _____	7 x 11 = _____	8 x 3 = _____
5 x 8 = _____	0 x 11 = _____	1 x 9 = _____	3 x 7 = _____
3 x 11 = _____	8 x 12 = _____	9 x 11 = _____	10 x 9 = _____
11 x 11 = _____	3 x 3 = _____	1 x 10 = _____	10 x 10 = _____
6 x 6 = _____	4 x 9 = _____	7 x 3 = _____	1 x 5 = _____
6 x 9 = _____	3 x 10 = _____	9 x 12 = _____	5 x 9 = _____
3 x 5 = _____	5 x 2 = _____	8 x 6 = _____	6 x 12 = _____
6 x 7 = _____	2 x 10 = _____	3 x 12 = _____	8 x 4 = _____
5 x 5 = _____	3 x 2 = _____	5 x 6 = _____	4 x 11 = _____
12 x 12 = _____	2 x 8 = _____	4 x 2 = _____	3 x 6 = _____
7 x 9 = _____	10 x 11 = _____	8 x 8 = _____	4 x 8 = _____
7 x 4 = _____	6 x 3 = _____	7 x 7 = _____	1 x 12 = _____
9 x 5 = _____	8 x 10 = _____	5 x 12 = _____	12 x 11 = _____
7 x 8 = _____	5 x 1 = _____	6 x 2 = _____	4 x 8 = _____
0 x 10 = _____	4 x 10 = _____	2 x 12 = _____	12 x 10 = _____

NAME _____ DATE _____

SCORE _____

100 DIVISION FACTS SPEED TEST

DIRECTIONS: Building your speed in knowing your division facts can help you improve your computation skills. Try to complete as many of these as you can in 5-10 minutes and then practice those that are difficult for you.

$56 \div 7 =$ _____	$42 \div 7 =$ _____	$72 \div 6 =$ _____	$16 \div 8 =$ _____
$96 \div 12 =$ _____	$22 \div 11 =$ _____	$64 \div 8 =$ _____	$99 \div 11 =$ _____
$27 \div 3 =$ _____	$84 \div 12 =$ _____	$45 \div 5 =$ _____	$132 \div 12 =$ _____
$32 \div 4 =$ _____	$24 \div 6 =$ _____	$36 \div 12 =$ _____	$55 \div 11 =$ _____
$60 \div 6 =$ _____	$12 \div 3 =$ _____	$121 \div 11 =$ _____	$108 \div 12 =$ _____
$6 \div 3 =$ _____	$28 \div 4 =$ _____	$88 \div 8 =$ _____	$77 \div 11 =$ _____
$81 \div 9 =$ _____	$24 \div 4 =$ _____	$35 \div 5 =$ _____	$100 \div 10 =$ _____
$18 \div 2 =$ _____	$144 \div 12 =$ _____	$18 \div 3 =$ _____	$8 \div 4 =$ _____
$48 \div 12 =$ _____	$42 \div 6 =$ _____	$12 \div 2 =$ _____	$54 \div 9 =$ _____
$24 \div 3 =$ _____	$120 \div 10 =$ _____	$5 \div 1 =$ _____	$15 \div 5 =$ _____
$50 \div 5 =$ _____	$44 \div 4 =$ _____	$20 \div 4 =$ _____	$110 \div 11 =$ _____
$40 \div 8 =$ _____	$54 \div 6 =$ _____	$60 \div 10 =$ _____	$80 \div 10 =$ _____
$88 \div 11 =$ _____	$48 \div 4 =$ _____	$44 \div 11 =$ _____	$56 \div 8 =$ _____
$72 \div 8 =$ _____	$132 \div 11 =$ _____	$90 \div 10 =$ _____	$77 \div 7 =$ _____
$63 \div 9 =$ _____	$6 \div 2 =$ _____	$24 \div 8 =$ _____	$18 \div 6 =$ _____
$70 \div 10 =$ _____	$16 \div 2 =$ _____	$21 \div 7 =$ _____	$35 \div 7 =$ _____
$55 \div 5 =$ _____	$36 \div 9 =$ _____	$33 \div 11 =$ _____	$24 \div 12 =$ _____
$0 \div 12 =$ _____	$120 \div 12 =$ _____	$60 \div 12 =$ _____	$70 \div 7 =$ _____
$36 \div 4 =$ _____	$30 \div 10 =$ _____	$10 \div 5 =$ _____	$49 \div 7 =$ _____
$4 \div 2 =$ _____	$96 \div 8 =$ _____	$60 \div 5 =$ _____	$80 \div 8 =$ _____
$14 \div 7 =$ _____	$30 \div 5 =$ _____	$40 \div 4 =$ _____	$24 \div 2 =$ _____
$16 \div 4 =$ _____	$66 \div 11 =$ _____	$72 \div 12 =$ _____	$40 \div 5 =$ _____
$28 \div 7 =$ _____	$20 \div 5 =$ _____	$20 \div 10 =$ _____	$108 \div 9 =$ _____
$9 \div 3 =$ _____	$12 \div 4 =$ _____	$36 \div 6 =$ _____	$50 \div 10 =$ _____
$48 \div 6 =$ _____	$27 \div 9 =$ _____	$25 \div 5 =$ _____	$36 \div 3 =$ _____

89

Page 1   1. 2 2. 4 3. 3 4. 6 5. 9 6. 1 7. 8 8. 0 9. 7 10. 5 (Their pen pals)

Page 2   1. 6,239 2. 1,399 3. 33,782 4. 576,832 5. 107,640 6. 684,000 7. 99,999 8. 9,500 9. 999,999
10. 6,750 11. 51,600 12. 3,678,000,000 13. 29,999 (The stalk brought you)

Page 3   1. 80,000 2. 75,400 3. 75,000 4. 75,420 5. 293,678,430 6. 293,678,400 7. 293,680,000
8. 293,678,000 9. 293,700,000 10. 290,000,000 11. 294,000,000 (You would eat fast food)

Page 4   1. 7,240,006 2. 42,364,030,400 3. 277,643,200,006 4. 70,000,024,060 5. 42,364,034 6. 277,643
7. 7,240,600,000 8. 277,643,600 9. 70,246 (Iguana go home)

Page 5   Answers will vary.

Page 6   Answers will vary.

Page 7   1. 110 2. 882 3. 155 4. 90 5. 431 6. 66 7. 510 8. 952 9. 148 10. 154 11. 143 12. 548 13. 131
(It's been nice gnawing you)

Page 8   1. 777 2. 109 3. 888 4. 587 5. 10,069 6. 3,324 7. $2205.39 8. 14,615 9. $19.12 10. 456
11. $54.10 12. 36,609 (Turkeys, monkeys, and donkeys)

Page 9   1. 18 2. 15 3. 27 4. 66 5. 56 6. 74 7. 76 8. 23 9. 65 10. 55 11. 13 (One is too thin and the other is
tooth out)

Page 10 1. 5,688 2. 3,359 3. 24,539 4. 1,879 5. 5,203 (Ooohm papa)

Page 11 Answers will vary.

Page 12 1. 2,131 2. 447 3. 6,774 4. 407 5. $35.21 6. 38,996 7. 463 8. 2,499 9. 3 10. 771,114 11. 387
12. 4,199 13. $101.11 (Awfully big hands)

Page 13 1. 932 2. 2,811 3. 4,523 4. 864 5. 802 6. 2,099 7. 1,459 8. 791 9. $15.85 10. $13.19
(A purr-snatcher)

Page 14 Answers will vary.

Page 19 1. 56 2. 21 3. 54 4. 36 5. 8 6. 7 7. 4 8. 6 9. 657 10. 384 11. 4,170 12. 2,569

Page 21 1. 6 x 8 = 48 or 8 x 8 = 64 2. 3 x 9 = 27 3. 4 x 4 = 16 4. 8 x 9 = 72 5. 9 x 9 = 81 6. 7 x 5 = 35
7. 7 x 7 = 49 8. 2 x 8 = 16 9. 5 x 6 = 30 10. 4 x 3 = 12 11. 7 x 9 = 63 12. 4 x 5 = 20 13. 7 x 8 = 56
14. 5 x 9 = 45 15. 3 x 6 = 18 16. 6 x 4 = 24

Page 22

1.

5	1	5
2	■	4
10	2	20

2.

5	2	10
1	■	3
5	6	30

3.

2	2	4
5	■	5
10	2	20

4.

3	2	6
1	■	4
3	8	24

5.

7	4	28
7	■	0
49	0	0

6.

7	4	28
2	■	1
14	2	28

7.

3	2	6
3	■	3
9	2	18

8.

8	9	72
3	■	1
24	3	72

Page 26 1. 78 2. 134 3. 105 4. 121 5. 147 6. 136 7. 122 8. 101 9. 296 10. 54 11. 160 12. 21
(You find the letter "e")

Page 27 1. 238 2. 2,608 3. 100 4. 1,071 5. 1,446 6. 105 7. 6,930 8. 285 9. 398 10. 410 11. 1,600
12. 4,912 (Chocolate chirp cookies)

Page 28 1. 2,052 2. 11,151 3. 2,480 4. 1,782 5. 45,372 6. 4,085 7. 5,994 8. 50,853 9. 4,588
10. 12,516 11. 3,752 (They eat what bugs them)

Page 29 1. 2,936 2. 592,816 3. 344,448 4. 1,986,096 5. 13,095 6. 5,515,888

Page 30 1. 281 R2 2. 1,355 R1 3. 130 R6 4. 1,568 R3 5. 404 R1 6. 608 R4 7. 3,162 8. 1,183 R6
9. $9.19 10. 500 R1 (You'd have bamboo)

Page 31 1. 99 2. 28 3. 691 4. 941 5. 49 6. 95 7. 97 8. 249 9. 98 10. 551 11. 382 12. 34
13. 15 (A river that's too big for its bridges)

Page 32 1. 56 2. 39 3. 32 4. 62 5. 97 6. 85 7. 13 8. 24 9. 43 10. 11 11. 156 (Through cow-ledge)

Page 33 1. 4 2. 0.432 3. 9.36 4. 162 5. $26 6. 94 7. 70 8. 18 9. 15 (A nightmare)

Page 36 1. 4,200 2. 82 3. 7,000 4. 60 5. 9 6. 3 7. 12,600 8. 96 9. 730,000 10. 5 11. 13,989 (To improve his bite)

Page 37 2. 60 x 1, 2 x 30, 3 x 20, 4 x 15, 5 x 12, 6 x 10 3. 48 x 1, 2 x 24, 3 x 16, 4 x 12, 6 x 8 4. 72 x 1, 2 x 36, 3 x 24, 4 x 18, 6 x 12, 8 x 9 5. 100 x 1, 2 x 50, 4 x 25, 5 x 20, 10 x 10 6. 32 x 1, 2 x 16, 4 x 8 7. 120 x 1, 2 x 60, 3 x 40, 4 x 30, 5 x 24, 6 x 20, 8 x 15, 10 x 12 8. 20 x 1, 10 x 2, 4 x 5 9. 80 x 1, 2 x 40, 4 x 20, 5 x 16, 10 x 8 10. 200 x 1, 2 x 100, 4 x 50, 5 x 40, 10 x 20, 8 x 25 11. 42 x 1, 2 x 21, 3 x 14, 7 x 6 12. 54 x 1, 2 x 27, 3 x 18, 6 x 9 13. 88 x 1, 2 x 44, 4 x 22, 8 x 11

Page 38 1. 20, Composite 2. 17, Prime 3. 33, Composite 4. 36, Composite 5. 11, Prime 6. 15, Composite 7. 29, Prime 8. 13, Prime 9. 112, Composite 10. 47, Prime 11. 87, Composite 12. 99, Composite 13. 83, Prime 14. 48, Composite 15. 93, Composite 16. 57, Composite 17. 49, Composite 18. 100, Composite 19. 41, Prime 20. 71, Prime

Page 39 1. $(3 \times 3) \times 3 = 27$ 2. $(5 \times 2) \times 3 = 30$ 3. $(5 \times 2) \times 5 = 50$ 4. $(5 \times 2) \times 2 = 20$ 5. $(5 \times 2) \times (3 \times 2) = 60$ 6. $(5 \times 3) \times 3 = 45$ 7. $(2 \times 3) \times (2 \times 2) \times 2 = 48$ 8. $(3 \times 3) \times (2 \times 2) \times 2 = 72$

Page 40 1. 6, 12, $\frac{1}{2}$ 2. 6, 72, $\frac{3}{4}$ 3. 5, 30, $\frac{2}{3}$ 4. 4, 48, $\frac{3}{4}$ 5. 2, 306, $\frac{9}{17}$ 6. 3, 36, $\frac{3}{4}$ 7. 10, 60, $\frac{2}{3}$ 8. 18, 36, $\frac{1}{2}$ 9. 5, 350, $\frac{5}{14}$ 10. 22, 44, $\frac{1}{2}$, 11. 17, 34, $\frac{1}{2}$ 12. 6, 144, $\frac{3}{8}$ 13. 12, 120, $\frac{2}{5}$ 14. 1, 1160, $\frac{29}{40}$ 15. 25, 100, $\frac{1}{4}$ 16. 15, 60, $\frac{1}{4}$

Page 43 1. $\frac{9}{10}$ 2. $\frac{3}{4}$ 3. $\frac{3}{8}$ 4. $\frac{2}{7}$ 5. $\frac{7}{8}$ 6. $\frac{17}{38}$ 7. $\frac{9}{20}$ 8. $\frac{3}{7}$ 9. $\frac{19}{28}$ 10. $\frac{17}{20}$ 11. $\frac{11}{28}$ 12. $\frac{7}{10}$ 13. $\frac{5}{8}$ (One wrong turn and you're in hot water)

Page 44 1. $\frac{5}{9}$ 2. $\frac{2}{7}$ 3. $\frac{3}{4}$ 4. $\frac{5}{6}$ 5. $\frac{1}{2}$ 6. $\frac{1}{3}$ 7. $\frac{7}{13}$ 8. $\frac{3}{5}$ 9. $\frac{1}{9}$ 10. $\frac{1}{6}$ 11. $\frac{2}{3}$ 12. $\frac{7}{10}$ (They use collie-flour)

Page 45 1. $1\frac{3}{4}$ 2. $1\frac{1}{2}$ 3. 2 4. $3\frac{1}{3}$ 5. $1\frac{3}{11}$ 6. $1\frac{3}{8}$ 7. 3 8. $4\frac{1}{5}$ 9. $4\frac{1}{2}$ 10. $2\frac{1}{2}$ 11. $1\frac{1}{3}$ (It's March fourth)

Page 46 1. $\frac{22}{5}$ 2. $\frac{17}{2}$ 3. $\frac{31}{3}$ 4. $\frac{8}{3}$ 5. $\frac{15}{4}$ 6. $\frac{38}{5}$ 7. $\frac{35}{6}$ 8. $\frac{11}{3}$ 9. $\frac{11}{6}$ 10. $\frac{27}{4}$ 11. $\frac{17}{7}$ 12. $\frac{46}{11}$ 13. $\frac{6}{5}$ (An icicle built for two)

Page 47 1. $\frac{1}{3}$ 2. $\frac{3}{20}$ 3. $\frac{1}{6}$ 4. $\frac{1}{21}$ 5. $\frac{5}{32}$ 6. $\frac{1}{4}$ 7. $\frac{9}{80}$ 8. $\frac{5}{12}$ 9. $\frac{1}{2}$ 10. $\frac{6}{25}$ 11. $\frac{3}{8}$ 12. $\frac{1}{9}$ 13. $\frac{5}{21}$ 14. $\frac{7}{10}$ (Sorry, we didn't planet this way)

Page 48 1. $7\frac{1}{3}$ 2. $9\frac{1}{3}$ 3. 56 4. $5\frac{2}{5}$ 5. $5\frac{1}{2}$ 6. $18\frac{1}{3}$ 7. $5\frac{1}{3}$ (You see Europe)

Page 49 1. 6 2. 9 3. 4 4. 15 5. 16 6. 1 7. 12 8. 2 9. 24 10. 14 11. 18 12. 3 13. 8 (I can't believe my census)

Page 50 1. $2\frac{1}{4}$ 2. $1\frac{13}{25}$ 3. 7 4. $3\frac{1}{2}$ 5. 16 6. 4 7. 2 8. $\frac{4}{9}$ 9. 6 10. $4\frac{1}{6}$ 11. $\frac{1}{2}$ 12. $1\frac{1}{6}$ 13. $1\frac{9}{13}$ 14. $1\frac{47}{88}$ Card 3 – $3\frac{1}{2}$ $\frac{1}{2}$ $1\frac{13}{25}$

Page 52 1. 7.8 2. 3.4 3. 12.05 4. 0.8 5. 100.007 6. 99.03 7. 40.45 8. 3.1 9. 4,000.2 10. 7.08 11. 0.008 12. 4.45 13. 90.3 14. 117.5 15. 33.004 (Take the words right out of his mouth)

Page 53 1. 4 2. 3 3. 9 4. 0 5. 7 6. 1 7. 8 8. 2 (A Lawn Moo-er)

Page 54 ACROSS A– 38, C-542, F– 6, G-908, J-3, K-752, N-61, P-3, Q-6, R-907, U-8903, Y-75, DOWN A-36, B-8, C-502 D-48, E-2, G-9560, J-3175, K-7, N-607, P-38, R-9, V-9, X-3

Page 55 1. 3.8 2. 44.1 3. 7.01 4. 1.00 5. 78.34 6. 66.71 7. 3.01 8. 5.25 9. 33.9 10. 14.1 11. 3.1 12. 6,351 13. 99 14. 1,001 15. 1.1 16. 0.4 (You get windshield vipers)

Page 56 1. 02 2. 32.7 3. 2.438 4. 9.262 5. 75.56 6. 555.2 7. 90.66 8. 64.63

Page 57 1. 15.7928 2. 9.953 3. 8.549 4. 38.773 5. .89 6. 4.009 7. 4457.548 (Shredded tweet)

Page 58 1. 26.41 2. 19.93 3. 7.36 4. 2.993 5. 9.205 6. $1.02 7. 8.7 8. 22.3 9. $6.79 10. $5.11 11. 3.65 12. 25.35 13. $20.07

Page 59 1. 3.765 2. .06972 3. 30.72 4. 17.78 5. 5.304 6. 1,444.12 7. 4.344 8. 31.678 9. 286.72 10. 15.648 11. 78 12. .0864 (A turtle on a skateboard)

Page 60 1. 9.7 2. 8.154 3. .052 4. 1.7 5. .244 6. 2.89 7. 2.560 8. 1.579 9. 2.26 10. 11.15 11. .008 12. .642 13. 3.03 14. .24 (I think I am coming down with something)

Page 61 1. 1.85 2. 125 3. 7.5 4. 0.33 5. 562 6. 0.67 7. 210 8. 0.71 9. 41.44 10. 1.07 11. 350 12. 7.32 (His bark was worse than his bite)

Page 62 10 Points, Across: Orange or Blue, Orange, Green , Orange, Blue
20 Points, Across: Orange, Blue, Blue, Green, Green,
30 Points, Across: Blue, Green, Blue, Orange, Blue
40 Points, Across: Orange or Blue, Green, Green, Blue, Orange
50 Points, Across: Green, Orange, Blue, Orange, Blue (Answers may vary according to the strategies students use to estimate)

91

Page 64 1. Answers will vary 2. 6 pairs of Fried Mosquito Wings 3. Barbecued Raccoon Ribs, Roadside Salad, Turtle Soup, Sweet Puddle Diet Drink, Skunk Flavored Popsicle 4. 2 orders of 20 Chocolate Covered Frog Legs because 2 x 4 = $8.00 as opposed to 4 orders at $2.25 each = $9.00. 5. No, the total for the 5 items is $7.90. 6. No, the cost is $28.09, Tax- $1.97, Total Cost- $30.06

Page 65 1. 3 2. 25 3. 18 4. 35 5. 14 6. 30 7. 40 8. 50 9. 80 10. 12 11. 16 12. 22 13. 28 14. 10 (I have more dates than you do)

Page 66 1. $\frac{3}{1}$ 2. $\frac{1}{2}$ 3. $\frac{2}{3}$ 4. $\frac{5}{6}$ 5. $\frac{5}{4}$ 6. $\frac{2}{5}$ 7. $\frac{1}{1}$ 8. $\frac{3}{2}$ (Ape Lincoln)

Page 67 1. 42% 2. 50% 3. 20% 4. 54% 5. 9% 6. 41% 7. 100% 8. 78% (To rock concerts)

Page 68 1. $\frac{1}{10}$ 2. $\frac{2}{5}$ 3. $\frac{7}{20}$ 4. $\frac{4}{5}$ 5. $\frac{3}{25}$ 6. $\frac{1}{50}$ 7. $\frac{13}{100}$ 8. $\frac{1}{4}$ 9. $\frac{3}{5}$ 10. $\frac{1}{100}$ (The Wrong Brothers)

Page 69 1. $4.00 2. $15.20 3. $8.25 4. $8.50 5. $4.95 6. $18.75 7. $40.00 8. $2.40 (Well, halo there)

Page 70 Team 1 – 62.4, 60.08, 60.58, 62.3, Total – 245.36 Team 2 – 63.4 62.4, 69.7, 66.35, Total – 261.85 Team 3 – 61.09, 65.6, 60.23, 64.75, Total – 251.67 Team 4 – 58.07, 64.4, 59.2, 55.88, Total – 237.55 Team 5 – 59.16, 57.36, 61.39, 59.76, Total – 237.67 (The winner is Team 4 by .12 over Team 5)

Page 71 1. 2 2. 16 3. 16 4. 2 5. 1 6. 4 7. 8 8. 8

Page 73 1. cm 2. km 3. mm 4. km 5. m 6. mm 7. m or cm 8. cm or mm 9. m 10. km 11. mL 12. L 13. L 14. mL 15. mL 16. L 17. L 18. mL 19. mg 20. kg 21. kg 22. g 23. mg 24. kg 25. kg 26. mg

Page 74 1. 87 2. 112 3. 84 4. 24 5. 26 6. 13 7. 40 8. 3 9. 22 10. 195 11. 13,000 (A chicken on one crutch)

Page 76 1. 46° 2. 120° 3. 55° 4. 26° 5. 130° 6. 69° 7. 29° 8. 166° 9. 13° 10. 180°

Page 78 1. 216 cubic feet 2. 30.25 square meters 3. 31.875 square inches 4. 96 cubic feet 5. 144 square centimeters 6. 27 cubic inches 7. 10 square units 8. 54.76 square meters 9. 18 cubic yards (Hare tonic)

Page 79 1. 54.4 m 2. 26.4 cm 3. 18 ft. 4. 42 yd. 5. 14.5 cm 6. 44 m 7. 28.8 ft. 8. 48 cm 9. 45 yd. (Look ma, no hands)

Page 85 Column 1: 18, 0, 17, 13, 5, 11, 12, 10, 6, 9, 14, 5, 12, 14, 3, 7, 11, 16, 11, 9, 7, 7, 9, 11, 5
Column 2: 9, 11, 10, 13, 15, 10, 6, 10, 16, 13, 10, 7, 2, 12, 8, 15, 7, 10, 3, 7, 8, 12, 11, 8, 8
Column 3: 3, 6, 4, 12, 13, 8, 9, 5, 17, 9, 11, 1, 12, 11, 14, 6, 9, 8, 4, 9, 6, 4, 13, 13, 6
Column 4: 16, 2, 5, 15, 14, 7, 14, 4, 8, 5, 6, 8, 5, 10, 8, 12, 10, 12, 4, 8, 12, 9, 6, 2, 11

Page 86 Column 1: 7, 4, 0, 3, 9, 1, 6, 8, 3, 4, 2, 5, 8, 8, 7, 8, 6, 3, 2, 1, 5, 3, 9, 0, 6
Column 2: 3, 2, 9, 8, 9, 9, 7, 2, 0, 4, 2, 5, 9, 9, 6, 7, 3, 6, 7, 7, 0, 5, 2, 1, 7
Column 3: 3, 3, 6, 2, 2, 2, 5, 6, 6, 9, 5, 9, 1, 1, 1, 5, 8, 4, 1, 5, 4, 4, 0, 8, 0
Column 4: 9, 3, 1, 5, 4, 4, 7, 7, 8, 6, 3, 0, 1, 0, 6, 4, 0, 2, 4, 0, 1, 9, 7, 5, 8

Page 87 Column 1: 0, 60, 48, 88, 2, 36, 22, 24, 48, 8, 54, 40, 33, 121, 36, 54, 15, 42, 25, 144, 63, 28, 45, 56, 0
Column 2: 27, 8, 24, 72, 70, 4, 84, 28, 12, 20, 30, 0, 96, 9, 36, 30, 10, 20, 6, 16, 110, 18, 80, 5, 40
Column 3: 81, 11, 50, 0, 55, 14, 24, 14, 15, 72, 77, 9, 99, 10, 21, 108, 48, 36, 30, 8, 64, 49, 60, 12, 24
Column 4: 56, 18, 40, 6, 0, 42, 12, 16, 35, 66, 24, 21, 90, 100, 5, 45, 72, 32, 44, 18, 32, 12, 132, 32, 120

Page 88 Column 1: 8, 8, 9, 8, 10, 2, 9, 9, 4, 8, 10, 5, 8, 9, 7, 7, 11, 0, 9, 2, 2, 4, 4, 3, 8
Column 2: 6, 2, 7, 4, 4, 7, 6, 12, 7, 12, 11, 9, 12, 12, 3, 8, 4, 10, 3, 12, 6, 6, 4, 3, 3
Column 3: 12, 8, 9, 3, 11, 11, 7, 6, 6, 5, 5, 6, 4, 9, 3, 3, 3, 5, 2, 12, 10, 6, 2, 6, 5
Column 4: 3, 9, 11, 5, 9, 7, 10, 2, 6, 3, 10, 8, 7, 11, 3, 5, 2, 10, 7, 10, 12, 8, 12, 5, 12